CountryLiving

farmhouse
★ KITCHEN ★
COOKBOOK

100 FRESH, EASY & DELICIOUS RECIPES

The Editors of Country Living

HEARST
books

CONTENTS

STOCK YOUR FARMHOUSE PANTRY

Doesn't it seem like almost every food craze—canning, pickling, farm-to-table, even moonshine—takes root in the country? But sorting through hundreds of grocery store offerings for the perfect pantry ingredients (with a country flair!) can seem like a daunting task. So we've done the work for you and compiled a concise list of condiments and ingredients you might not normally have on hand. Try them for new flavor twists in your home cooking!

BARREL-AGED SORGHUM
Dress up biscuits with this rich maple syrup substitute.

BLACK TRUFFLE SALT
You know that truffle fries smell? Add a similarly intoxicating aroma to any dish with this indulgence.

CIDER VINEGAR
Kick your salad dressing game up a notch with this super-crisp apple vinegar.

DILLY BEANS
Pickled green beans add a country kick to a cheese plate.

FLAKED COCONUT
The subtle sweetness and texture of coconut can be utilized in both sweet and savory dishes.

HOT SAUCE
A little goes a long way when you're looking to add some extra spice.

LEMON CURD
This not-too-tart curd with an extra silky texture is just the thing to serve up with a few cookies.

OLD-FASHIONED COCKTAIL
This pre-bottled concoction tastes like it was whipped up by a real-deal, suspender-wearin' bartender.

PANKO BREAD CRUMBS
This Japanese-style bread crumb is super-crunchy and crispy and holds up well as a coating for meats, veggies, and more.

QUINOA CEREAL
This of-the-moment ancient grain now comes in pop cereal form! Serve it over yogurt for extra crunch.

SALSA
This spiced chunky sauce is more than a chip's sidekick—it can be added to a number of recipes to add just the right jolt of flavor.

SESAME OIL
This oil infuses a delicious, nutty flavor whenever used.

TACO SEASONING
This collection of spices isn't limited to Taco Tuesday—it can be used to infuse flavor in lots of other dishes!

TEA CONCENTRATE
Add water or your favorite spirit.

WHOLE-GRAIN FETTUCCINE
The nutty flavor and texture adds a new (and healthy!) dimension to everyday pasta dishes.

WILDFLOWER HONEY
This robust, floral-nectar honey is perfect for baking or sweetening your morning cup of coffee.

CHAPTER
ONE

– upgrade your –

MORNING ROUTINE

SLOW-COOKER PORRIDGE

Packed with whole grains (oats, quinoa, barley), this hearty, hands-off recipe will become your morning go-to. Top it any way you wish.

ACTIVE TIME: 10 minutes
TOTAL TIME: 8 hours 10 minutes
MAKES: 8 servings

1	cup steel-cut oats
½	cup red quinoa
½	cup brown rice
½	cup pearled barley
4	cups whole milk
¾	teaspoon salt
7 ½	cups water
2	tablespoons unsalted butter

In greased 6-quart slow-cooker bowl, stir together oats, quinoa, brown rice, pearled barley, milk, salt, and water. Cover and cook until grains are tender, on high for 3 to 4 hours or on low for 7 to 8 hours. Stir in butter. Serve with desired toppings.

Variations

➤➤ Grated Cheddar cheese, crumbled bacon, chopped dates, and sliced chives

➤➤ Sliced bananas, sliced red grapes, and dollop of peanut butter

➤➤ Fried egg, smoked salmon, sliced scallions, capers, and black pepper

➤➤ Fresh figs, toasted pistachios, pinch of ground nutmeg, and drizzle of honey

➤➤ Sliced oranges, toasted coconut, toasted pecans, and ground cinnamon

PINEAPPLE, GINGER & WALNUT OATMEAL

Zesty ginger and juicy pineapple give basic baked oatmeal an unexpected flair.

ACTIVE TIME: 5 minutes
TOTAL TIME: 30 minutes
MAKES: 4 servings

2	cups old-fashioned rolled oats
2	cups coarsely chopped fresh pineapple
1	cup coarsely chopped walnuts
1	(2-inch) piece fresh ginger, peeled and grated (about 2 tablespoons)
½	teaspoon salt
2	cups whole milk
½	cup maple syrup, plus more for serving
2	large eggs, beaten
2	teaspoons pure vanilla extract

1 Preheat oven to 400°F. In large bowl, stir together oats, pineapple, walnuts, ginger, and salt. Divide mixture among four 10-ounce ramekins. Set aside.

2 In medium bowl, whisk together milk, maple syrup, eggs, and vanilla. Pour one-quarter of the milk-syrup mixture over the oat-pineapple mixture in each ramekin.

3 Transfer ramekins to baking sheet. Bake until oats are set and lightly golden brown on top, about 25 minutes. Serve with extra maple syrup on the side.

SPRING VEGETABLE, HAM & GOAT CHEESE FRITTATA

This brunch-ready dish is perfect for feeding a hungry crowd.

ACTIVE TIME: 20 minutes
TOTAL TIME: 35 minutes
MAKES: 8 servings

8	large eggs
3/4	cup heavy cream
3	ounces ham, chopped
1	teaspoon salt
1/2	teaspoon black pepper
2	tablespoons unsalted butter
1/2	pound asparagus, trimmed and cut into 2-inch pieces
6	radishes, thinly sliced
4	scallions, sliced
1	garlic clove, finely chopped
4	ounces goat cheese, crumbled

1 Preheat oven to 350°F. In bowl, whisk together eggs, cream, ham, salt, and pepper.

2 In 10-inch ovenproof nonstick skillet, melt butter over medium-high heat. Add asparagus and sauté until tender-crisp, 2 to 4 minutes. Add radishes, scallions, and garlic and sauté until scallions are just wilted, 1 to 2 minutes.

3 Reduce heat to medium. Pour egg mixture over vegetables and cook until eggs begin to set around the edges, 3 to 4 minutes. Sprinkle with goat cheese.

4 Transfer to oven and bake until set, 15 to 17 minutes. Serve immediately.

Eggs 101

Follow these simple steps to make the perfect egg every time!

★ HARD-BOILED

1 Place 4 eggs in a medium pot and fill with enough cold water to cover eggs by 1 inch. Place pot over high heat and bring water to a boil. Remove pot from heat and allow to sit, covered, for 12 minutes.

2 Pour off water and run eggs under cold water to cool.

3 Tap eggs on work surface, then gently roll to loosen shell. Peel off shell.

★ SCRAMBLED

1 In a medium bowl, whisk 4 eggs, 1 to 2 tablespoons cream or milk, until light and frothy, add salt and black pepper to taste.

2 In a 10- or 12-inch nonstick skillet, melt ½ to 1 tablespoon butter over low heat until bubbly.

3 Pour egg mixture into center of pan. As egg starts to set, use a heatproof spatula to scrape cooked egg into the center. Repeat, scraping and folding, until no liquid remains and moist curds form. Transfer to a warm plate and adjust seasonings; serve immediately.

★ POACHED

1 Crack 1 egg into each of four ramekins. In a large straight-sided skillet, bring 2 to 3 inches slightly salted water and 1 teaspoon white vinegar to a simmer over medium-high heat.

2 Carefully slide one egg at a time into water, spacing evenly.

3 Partially cover pan and poach until white is firm (not runny) and yolk is opaque, 3 ½ to 4 ½ minutes. With a slotted spoon, remove eggs and season with salt and pepper; serve immediately.

POTATO & MANCHEGO CASSEROLE WITH MAPLE BACON

Cheese, potatoes, and maple bacon will satisfy all your morning cravings.

ACTIVE TIME: 20 minutes
TOTAL TIME: 1 hour 45 minutes
MAKES: 8 servings

2	pounds fingerling potatoes
12	ounces applewood-smoked bacon, cut into 1-inch pieces
¼	cup maple syrup
½	teaspoon cayenne pepper
	Butter, for baking dish
2	cups shredded Manchego cheese
5	scallions, white and green parts chopped
6	large eggs, beaten
1	cup whole milk
½	teaspoon salt
½	teaspoon black pepper

1 Preheat oven to 350°F. In medium pot, cover potatoes with water and bring to a boil over medium heat. Reduce to a simmer; cook until potatoes are just tender, 10 to 15 minutes. Drain potatoes and let rest until cool enough to handle. Cut each in half lengthwise. Set aside.

2 In large skillet, cook bacon over medium-high heat until crisp, about 6 minutes per side. Remove skillet from heat and stir in maple syrup and cayenne. Set aside.

3 Butter 2-quart baking dish and set aside. In large bowl, stir together reserved potatoes, maple-bacon mixture, cheese, and scallions. Transfer to prepared baking dish. Set aside.

4 In large bowl, whisk together eggs, milk, salt, and pepper. Slowly pour over potato mixture. Bake until top is golden, about 50 minutes. Let casserole cool slightly before serving.

For a lighter version, replace bacon with chicken sausage, swap Manchego for low-fat Swiss, and use egg substitute to save 179 calories and 22 grams of fat per serving.

TWISTED STICKY CARAMEL-PECAN ROLL

You may want to make two of these gooey, sweet rolls, since it's bound to disappear in seconds!

ACTIVE TIME: 30 minutes
TOTAL TIME: 2 hours 45 minutes
MAKES: 8 servings

¼ cup (½ stick) unsalted butter, softened, plus more for pan

2 tablespoons plus ½ cup packed dark brown sugar, divided

3 ounces cream cheese, softened

½ cup finely chopped toasted pecans

1 ½ teaspoons ground cinnamon

¼ teaspoon salt

1 pound prepared pizza dough, at room temperature

Quick Caramel Glaze (recipe below)

1 Generously butter bottom and sides of 9-inch cast-iron skillet or cake pan. Sprinkle bottom of pan with 2 tablespoons brown sugar.

2 In bowl, stir together cream cheese and butter until smooth. In another bowl, stir together pecans, cinnamon, salt, and remaining ½ cup brown sugar.

3 Roll and stretch dough into 14-inch square (if dough springs back, cover with dish towel and let stand for 5 minutes before continuing to roll). Spread dough with cream cheese mixture and sprinkle sugar mixture on one half. Fold other half over sugar and press lightly to adhere. Cut dough lengthwise into 5 strips. Tightly twist each dough strip. Beginning in center of prepared pan, wrap strips in a spiral pattern, pinching ends together. Cover and let stand in warm, dry place for 45 minutes.

4 Preheat oven to 350°F. Bake until golden and cooked through, 30 to 32 minutes. Meanwhile, prepare Quick Caramel Glaze.

5 Transfer roll to a serving plate and drizzle with warm Quick Caramel Glaze. Serve warm.

★ QUICK CARAMEL GLAZE

In small saucepan, combine ¼ cup packed **dark brown sugar**, ¼ cup (½ stick) **unsalted butter**, and 3 tablespoons **cream**; bring to a boil over medium heat. Boil until sugar dissolves, 2 to 4 minutes, stirring constantly. Remove from heat and stir in 1 teaspoon **pure vanilla extract** and ¼ teaspoon ★ **salt**.

PERFECTLY BUTTERY CREAM SCONES

This slightly sweet scone will become your new go-to recipe. Add a sweet flavor twist with tangerine-rosemary, or keep them savory with the addition of feta or country ham.

ACTIVE TIME: 15 minutes
TOTAL TIME: 55 minutes
MAKES: 8 scones

2 ½ cups all-purpose flour, spooned and leveled
⅓ cup granulated sugar
1 tablespoon baking powder
½ teaspoon salt
½ cup (1 stick) cold unsalted butter, cut up
1 cup heavy whipping cream, divided
1 large egg, beaten

BUTTERMILK GLAZE
1 cup confectioners' sugar
2 tablespoons buttermilk
½ teaspoon pure vanilla extract

1 Preheat oven to 425°F. In bowl, whisk together flour, sugar, baking powder, and salt. Cut butter into flour mixture with two forks or pastry blender until crumbly and mixture resembles small peas. Freeze until butter is hard, 14 to 16 minutes. Add cream, stirring with fork just until dry ingredients are moistened. While in bowl, gently knead into a ball.

2 Turn dough out onto parchment-lined baking sheet. Pat dough into 8-inch circle (about ¾- to 1-inch thick). Cut into 8 wedges and space ½ inch apart. Brush with egg.

3 Bake, rotating baking sheet once, until golden brown and center is firm, 22 to 25 minutes. Transfer to wire rack; cool for 10 minutes.

4 Make Buttermilk Glaze: In bowl, whisk together confectioners' sugar, buttermilk, and vanilla until smooth. Drizzle over cooled scones.

Variations

TANGERINE-ROSEMARY:

Omit Buttermilk Glaze. Whisk
1 tablespoon **tangerine zest**,
⅓ cup **tangerine marmalade**,
and 1 tablespoon finely chopped
fresh rosemary into cream.
Microwave ¼ cup **tangerine
marmalade** and 1 teaspoon
finely chopped **fresh rosemary**
until just melted. Brush over
warm scones. Garnish with
1 small **rosemary sprig**.

SCALLION AND FETA:

Reduce granulated sugar to
2 tablespoons and omit
Buttermilk Glaze. Toss
3 thinly sliced **scallions**, 1 cup
crumbled **feta cheese**, and
2 teaspoons **cracked black
pepper** into flour mixture
before adding cream.

BLUEBERRY-LAVENDER:

Toss 6 ounces **blueberries**,
1 tablespoon **lemon zest**, and
2 teaspoons finely crushed

lavender blossoms into flour
mixture. Sprinkle glazed scones
with a few more lavender
blossoms.

HAM, JALAPEÑO, AND CHEDDAR:

Reduce granulated sugar to
2 tablespoons. Toss ½ cup
finely chopped **country ham**,
1 cup shredded **extra-sharp
Cheddar cheese**, and 1 minced
jalapeño into flour mixture.
Top dough wedges with **jalapeño
slices** before baking.

WHOLE-GRAIN BUTTERMILK PANCAKES

Mix the dry ingredients for Make-Ahead Whole-Grain Pancakes up to 2 months in advance. Come Saturday morning, stir in a few wet ingredients and breakfast is served!

TOTAL TIME: 25 minutes
MAKES: 4 servings

1 ½ cups Make-Ahead Whole-Grain Pancake Mix (recipe below)
1 ½ cups buttermilk
2 large eggs
3 tablespoons unsalted butter, melted, plus more for griddle

1 In large bowl, stir together pancake mix, buttermilk, eggs, and butter until just blended and smooth.

2 Heat griddle or large nonstick skillet over medium heat; butter. Pour about ¼ cup batter for each pancake onto griddle. Cook until tops are covered with bubbles and edges look dry, 2 to 4 minutes. Turn and cook until plump and cooked through, 2 to 3 minutes more. Place pancakes in single layer on baking sheet and keep warm in 175°F oven for up to 30 minutes. Repeat with remaining batter.

MAKE-AHEAD WHOLE-GRAIN PANCAKE MIX

Pulse 3 cups **quick-cooking oats** and ½ cup **flax seeds** in food processor until finely chopped, 10 to 15 times. In large bowl, stir together oat mixture, 3 cups (spooned and leveled) **white whole wheat flour**, 2 cups (spooned and leveled) **buckwheat flour**, 2 cups (spooned and leveled) **all-purpose flour**, ¼ cup **granulated sugar**, ¼ cup **baking powder**, 4 teaspoons **salt**, and 1 tablespoon **baking soda**. Store in airtight container in refrigerator or freezer for up to 2 months.

Variations

STRAWBERRY-POPPY SEED: 1 ½ cups sliced fresh strawberries, 2 tablespoons poppy seeds, and 1 ½ tablespoons each lemon zest and juice

APRICOT-GOAT CHEESE: ¾ cup diced dried apricots, ½ cup crumbled goat cheese, and 2 tablespoons each chopped fresh mint and honey

MANGO-COCONUT: 1 cup diced fresh mango, ¾ cup sweetened flaked coconut, ½ cup chopped roasted salted macadamia nuts, and 1 tablespoon lime zest

PEAR-WALNUT: 1 cup peeled diced ripe pear, ½ cup chopped toasted walnuts, and ¾ teaspoon ground cinnamon

ALMOND GRANOLA-CHOCOLATE: 1 cup almond granola and ¾ cup dark chocolate chips

PANCAKE BREAKFAST SANDWICHES WITH SAUSAGE & AVOCADO

Turn things up a notch and use fluffy pancakes as the bread in this yummy breakfast sandwich.

ACTIVE TIME: 40 minutes
TOTAL TIME: 55 minutes
MAKES: 4 sandwiches

1 ¾ cups all-purpose flour, spooned and leveled

4   teaspoons baking powder

2   teaspoons granulated sugar

½   teaspoon salt

1 ¼ cups whole milk

1   large egg

1   tablespoon unsalted butter, melted, plus more for griddle

¾   pound breakfast sausage, casing removed and shaped into 4 (3-inch) patties

1   avocado, sliced

4   large fried eggs

1 ½ cups baby arugula

1 In bowl, whisk together flour, baking powder, sugar, and salt. In separate bowl, whisk together milk, egg, and butter. Stir milk mixture into flour mixture just until blended and smooth. Let stand for 15 minutes.

2 Heat griddle or large nonstick skillet over medium heat; butter. Pour about ¼ cup batter for each pancake onto hot griddle. Cook until puffed, tops are covered with bubbles, and edges look dry, 3 to 4 minutes. Turn and cook until plump and cooked through, 2 to 3 minutes more. Place pancakes in single layer on baking sheet and keep warm in 175°F oven for up to 30 minutes. Repeat with remaining batter.

3 Wipe griddle clean with paper towel and increase heat to medium-high. Cook sausage until no longer pink in the middle, 3 to 4 minutes per side.

4 Top four pancakes with sausage, avocado, fried eggs, and arugula, dividing evenly. Top with remaining pancakes. Serve immediately.

For the perfect pancake, use a thin metal spatula held 3 inches above the griddle and a quick flick of the wrist!

GRAPEFRUIT BUTTERMILK DOUGHNUTS WITH ZEST

Tangy buttermilk and tart grapefruit lend an air of sophistication to this breakfast staple. And yes—they really do taste as good as they look.

ACTIVE TIME: 20 minutes
TOTAL TIME: 1 hour
MAKES: 12 doughnuts

2   cups all-purpose flour
2   cups granulated sugar
2   teaspoons baking powder
1   teaspoon ground ginger
½   teaspoon salt
1 ¼ cups buttermilk
1   large egg, lightly beaten
2   tablespoons canola oil
1   teaspoon pure vanilla extract
Zest of 1 large grapefruit, plus 4 (2-inch-long) strips grapefruit peel, thinly sliced
1   cup confectioners' sugar
3   tablespoons grapefruit juice

1 Preheat oven to 350°F. Coat two 6-cavity doughnut pans with cooking spray. In large bowl, combine flour, 1 ½ cups granulated sugar, baking powder, ginger, and salt and mix well. In small bowl, whisk together buttermilk, egg, oil, vanilla, and grapefruit zest. Add wet ingredients to dry ingredients and stir. Spoon batter into prepared pans, filling each cavity a little more than three-quarters full. Bake for 25 to 30 minutes. Let doughnuts cool in pan for 5 minutes, then turn out onto wire rack to cool completely.

2 In small bowl, whisk together confectioners' sugar and juice until smooth. Set glaze aside. In small saucepan, combine peel strips, 3 tablespoons granulated sugar, and 3 tablespoons water and bring to a boil. Reduce heat to low and simmer until sugar dissolves, about 5 minutes; strain. Toss peel immediately in remaining granulated sugar until coated. Transfer to cutting board and chop.

3 For each doughnut, carefully dip top in glaze, then set glaze-side up on wire rack so excess drips off. Sprinkle immediately with chopped candied zest.

CHAPTER
TWO

— fast & fresh —

FARM-TO-FORK

MUSHROOM & ASPARAGUS PIZZAS

What better way to eat fresh veggies than atop a light, crispy pizza?

ACTIVE TIME: 25 minutes
TOTAL TIME: 45 minutes
MAKES: 4 servings

4   tablespoons olive oil, divided, plus more for baking sheets
12   ounces mixed mushrooms (such as cremini, button, oyster, shiitake), thinly sliced
Salt and black pepper
1   pound pizza dough, at room temperature
4 to 5 asparagus stalks, thinly shaved
4   ounces fresh goat cheese, crumbled (about 1 cup)
4   ounces grated pecorino cheese (about 1 cup)
¼   teaspoon crushed red pepper
Mixed green salad, for serving

1 Preheat oven to 500°F with racks positioned in upper and lower thirds of oven. Oil two baking sheets.

2 In large skillet, heat 3 tablespoons oil over medium-high heat. Add mushrooms and season with salt and pepper. Cook until golden brown and tender, 8 to 10 minutes, stirring occasionally.

3 Divide dough into four pieces and stretch each into 7-inch circle; place on prepared baking sheets. Top evenly with mushrooms, asparagus, goat cheese, pecorino, and red pepper; season with salt and pepper. Brush edges of dough with remaining 1 tablespoon oil.

4 Bake, rotating the sheets front to back and top to bottom halfway through cooking, until the crust is golden brown, 10 to 12 minutes.

5 Serve pizzas with mixed green salad alongside.

CRUNCHY CARROT, PEA & CHICKEN SALAD

This fresh, crunchy salad gets a protein boost from no-fuss rotisserie chicken.

TOTAL TIME: 30 minutes
MAKES: 4 servings

⅓ loaf ciabatta bread, cut into 1-inch cubes
3 tablespoons olive oil
2 garlic cloves, minced
Salt and black pepper
½ pound baby rainbow carrots, halved lengthwise
6 cups torn Little Gem or romaine lettuce
2 cups shredded rotisserie chicken
1 cup cooked fresh or frozen peas
1 small fennel bulb, halved, cored, and thinly sliced
Mustard-Chive Vinaigrette (recipe below)

1 Preheat oven to 350°F. On a baking sheet, toss together bread, oil, and garlic; season with salt and pepper. Bake until bread cubes are golden brown and crisp, 10 to 12 minutes, stirring once.

2 In medium saucepan, cook carrots in boiling salted water over high heat until tender-crisp, 2 to 3 minutes. Drain and run under cold water until cool.

3 Gently toss together lettuce, shredded chicken, peas, fennel, croutons, carrots, and vinaigrette in a bowl; season with salt and pepper.

★ MUSTARD-CHIVE VINAIGRETTE

Whisk together ¼ cup **olive oil**, 2 tablespoons **white balsamic vinegar**, 1½ tablespoons chopped **fresh chives**, ½ small minced **shallot**, 1½ teaspoons **Dijon mustard**, and 1 teaspoon **granulated sugar**. Season with **salt** and **black pepper**. ★

BREADED PORK CUTLET WITH AVOCADO & SHREDDED KALE SALAD

Pork and avocado are a perfect pairing in this spring salad.

TOTAL TIME: 35 minutes
MAKES: 4 servings

1   large bunch Lacinato (Tuscan) kale, thick stems discarded and leaves thinly sliced
5   tablespoons olive oil, divided
Salt and black pepper
4   pork cutlets (about 1 pound total), pounded thin
¼   cup all-purpose flour
2   large eggs, beaten
1   cup panko bread crumbs
1   small head radicchio, leaves torn
1   cup snap peas, thinly sliced
1   avocado, chopped
1   lemon, peel removed and flesh chopped

1 In bowl, toss together kale and 3 tablespoons oil; season with salt and pepper. Set aside to soften.

2 Place flour in shallow dish. In second shallow dish, add eggs. In third shallow dish, add bread crumbs. Season pork with salt and pepper. Working one piece at a time, dip pork in flour, then in eggs, and then in bread crumbs, pressing gently to help adhere.

3 In large nonstick skillet, heat remaining 2 tablespoons oil over medium-high heat. Cook pork, in batches, until golden brown and cooked through, 2 to 3 minutes per side. Slice into thin strips.

4 Add radicchio, snap peas, avocado, and lemon to kale and toss to combine; season with salt and pepper.

5 Serve salad topped with pork.

Grow Your Own Salad Greens

The cost of store-bought radicchio can be radicch-ulous! So get to work sowing your own leafy supply.

There's no better motivation to eat more greens than growing them within 20 feet of your kitchen. And good news: Most are just as low-maintenance as your everyday herbs. Top picks: arugula, because it's spicy; red leaf, because it's mild and adds a nice splash of color to any salad; and romaine, because it's crunchy and pairs well with shaved Parmesan and lemon dressing. Set up your new crop in an old crate—it's the perfect vessel for sowing seeds in fertile, moist soil.

SPINACH & BARLEY SALAD WITH GRILLED PORK

Chock-full of seasonal veggies, this healthy, hearty dish will satisfy even the pickiest eater.

ACTIVE TIME: 25 minutes
TOTAL TIME: 40 minutes
MAKES: 6 servings

1	cup pearled barley
1	teaspoon salt
1	teaspoon black pepper
1	pork tenderloin (1 ¼ pounds)
1	tablespoon olive oil
6	cups baby spinach
4	large radishes, thinly sliced
3	baby chioggia (striped) or yellow beets, peeled and thinly sliced
3	scallions, sliced
2	medium carrots, thinly sliced
½	cup chopped toasted walnuts

Smoky Paprika Vinaigrette (recipe below)

1 In medium saucepan, cook barley in boiling salted water over medium-high heat until tender, 24 to 26 minutes. Drain and run under cold water until cool.

2 Prepare outdoor grill for covered direct grilling over medium-high heat. Rub pork with oil and season with salt and pepper. Cover and grill until the internal temperature registers 145°F, turning occasionally, 15 to 18 minutes. Remove to plate and allow to rest for 5 minutes before slicing.

3 In bowl, toss together spinach, radishes, beets, scallions, carrots, walnuts, barley, and vinaigrette; season with salt and pepper to taste.

4 Serve salad with sliced pork.

★ SMOKY PAPRIKA VINAIGRETTE

In small bowl, whisk together ½ cup **olive oil**, ¼ cup **red wine vinegar**, 1 ½ tablespoons **honey**, 2 teaspoons **Dijon mustard**, and 1 ¼ teaspoons **smoked paprika**. Season with **salt** and **black pepper**. Dressing can be stored in the refrigerator for up to 5 days. ★

HEIRLOOM TOMATO SANDWICHES

Though this sandwich is fresh and light, prosciutto keeps it satisfying and substantial.

ACTIVE TIME: 15 minutes
TOTAL TIME: 30 minutes
MAKES: 4 sandwiches

½ cup mayonnaise
1   garlic clove, minced
1   tablespoon chopped fresh tarragon
4   slices prosciutto (about 2 ounces)
4   slices white bread
4   tablespoons butter, softened
12 slices heirloom tomatoes
Sea salt and black pepper

1 Preheat oven to 350°F. In small bowl, combine mayonnaise, garlic, and tarragon. Set aside.

2 Place prosciutto on baking sheet and bake until crispy, 12 to 15 minutes. Set aside until cool enough to handle; break into small pieces.

3 Spread 1 slice bread with ½ tablespoon butter on each side; repeat for remaining 3 bread slices. In grill pan, grill bread over medium-high heat until golden and slightly charred, about 2 minutes per side.

4 To assemble each sandwich, spread 2 tablespoons reserved tarragon aioli on toasted bread. Layer on 3 slices tomatoes and top with crumbled prosciutto. Sprinkle with salt and pepper.

GREEK CHICKEN WITH TOMATO & RICE SALAD

This refreshing twist on chicken turns the usual into something unexpected (and delicious!). For photo, see page 4.

ACTIVE TIME: 20 minutes
TOTAL TIME: 40 minutes
MAKES: 4 servings

1 tablespoon finely grated lemon zest, plus 2 tablespoons fresh lemon juice
1 tablespoon chopped fresh thyme
1 ½ teaspoons Greek seasoning
5 tablespoons olive oil, divided
3 garlic cloves, minced and divided
4 boneless skinless chicken breasts (about 1 ½ pounds total)
⅓ cup dry white wine
1 cup royal rice blend
1 cup grape tomatoes, halved
3 small baby cucumbers, sliced
3 scallions, sliced
1 cup fresh flat-leaf parsley
¼ cup sliced fresh mint
2 ounces crumbled feta cheese (about ½ cup)

1 Preheat oven to 400°F.

2 In bowl, combine lemon zest, thyme, Greek seasoning, 2 tablespoons oil, and 2 garlic cloves. Rub mixture on chicken breasts. Pour wine into 11" by 7" baking dish and place chicken on top. Bake until chicken is cooked through and the internal temperature reaches 165°F, 28 to 30 minutes. Allow chicken to rest for 5 minutes before slicing.

3 Meanwhile, prepare rice according to package directions. Transfer rice to bowl and stir in tomatoes, cucumbers, scallions, parsley, mint, feta, lemon juice, remaining 3 tablespoons oil, and remaining 1 garlic clove.

4 Serve rice salad topped with chicken, warm or at room temperature.

SKILLET CHICKEN & SPRING VEGETABLES

For a slight recipe shake-up, feel free to swap in other spring veggies—try sliced baby carrots, green peas, or blanched new potatoes.

TOTAL TIME: 25 minutes
MAKES: 4 servings

4   boneless skinless chicken breasts (about 1 ½ pounds total)
1 ¼ teaspoons salt
¾   teaspoon black pepper
3   tablespoons cold unsalted butter, divided
1   large shallot, chopped
⅓   cup dry white wine
1 ½ cups snow peas
1 ½ cups sugar snap peas
1 ½ cups asparagus spears, sliced
1   large garlic clove, finely chopped
1 to 2 tablespoons chopped fresh tarragon
2   teaspoons lemon zest

1 Season chicken with salt and pepper. In large skillet, melt 1 tablespoon butter over medium-high heat. Add chicken and cook until deep golden brown, 4 to 6 minutes. Turn, reduce heat to medium, and cook until internal temperature reaches 165°F, 6 to 8 minutes. Remove to plate.

2 Increase heat to medium-high. Add shallot to skillet and cook until softened, about 1 minute. Stir in wine and cook, scraping brown bits from bottom of skillet, until reduced by three-quarters, 1 to 2 minutes. Stir in both peas and asparagus and sauté until just tender, 2 to 4 minutes. Stir in garlic and cook until fragrant, about 1 minute. Fold in tarragon and remaining 2 tablespoons butter; season with salt and pepper to taste.

3 Serve sprinkled with lemon zest.

SALT & PEPPER CHICKEN WITH SPRING QUINOA PILAF

Delicious and healthy join forces on a single plate in this bright summer dish.

ACTIVE TIME: 20 minutes
TOTAL TIME: 45 minutes
MAKES: 4 servings

¼ cup olive oil
8 small bone-in chicken thighs (about 1 ½ pounds total), skin on
Salt and black pepper
1 cup quinoa, rinsed
2 tablespoons unseasoned rice wine vinegar
4 scallions, sliced
3 radishes, halved and thinly sliced
1 small carrot, grated
3 ounces feta cheese, crumbled (about ¾ cup)
¼ cup fresh basil leaves, torn

1 Preheat oven to 450°F. In large ovenproof skillet, heat 2 tablespoons oil over medium-high heat. Season chicken with salt and pepper. Cook skin-side down, in batches, until skin is golden and crispy, 5 to 7 minutes. Return all chicken to skillet, skin-side up, and transfer skillet to oven. Roast until internal temperature of chicken reaches 165°F, 18 to 22 minutes.

2 Meanwhile, cook quinoa according to package directions. In bowl, whisk together vinegar and remaining 2 tablespoons oil. Add scallions, radishes, carrot, feta, basil, and quinoa and toss to combine.

3 Serve chicken over quinoa pilaf.

Tip

Can't find small chicken thighs?
Use four large ones and increase time in the oven to 25 to 30 minutes.

SALMON & BEETS WITH YOGURT SAUCE OVER WATERCRESS

The combo of fresh fish and a sweet, crunchy salad can't be beet.
For photo, see page 2.

TOTAL TIME: 25 minutes
MAKES: 4 servings

1 ¼ pounds beets (about 5 small), peeled and cut into 1-inch wedges
½ cup plain yogurt
2 tablespoons chopped fresh dill, plus more for serving
½ teaspoon lemon zest, plus 1 tablespoon lemon juice
1 tablespoon olive oil
1 tablespoon poppy seeds
Salt and black pepper
4 skinless salmon fillets (6 ounces each)
1 teaspoon ground coriander
1 bunch watercress, thick stems removed

1 In medium saucepan, set steamer basket over 1 inch boiling water.
Add beets and steam until tender, 18 to 20 minutes.

2 In bowl, whisk together yogurt, dill, lemon zest and juice, oil, and poppy
seeds; season with salt and pepper.

3 Preheat broiler. Season salmon with coriander, salt, and pepper. Place on
rimmed baking sheet and broil until just opaque throughout, 5 to 6 minutes.

4 Serve salmon, beets, and watercress topped with yogurt sauce.

SEARED GROUPER WITH CORN, ZUCCHINI & TOMATO SAUTÉ

Perfect for relaxing on a cool summer evening, this laid-back fish dish takes only 20 minutes to prepare.

TOTAL TIME: 20 minutes
MAKES: 4 servings

4	grouper fillets, or other firm fish such as halibut, cod, or salmon (6 ounces each)
1	teaspoon salt
½	teaspoon black pepper
2	tablespoons olive oil
2	medium zucchini, halved lengthwise and sliced
1	large shallot, chopped
1 ½	cups fresh yellow corn kernels (from 2 large ears)
2	garlic cloves, minced
1 ½	cups cherry tomatoes, halved
2	tablespoons cold butter, cubed
¼	cup torn basil leaves

1 Sprinkle fish with salt and pepper. In large nonstick skillet, heat oil over medium-high heat. Cook fish for 4 minutes on each side, until browned and cooked through. Remove and keep warm.

2 In same skillet, sauté zucchini and shallots for 4 minutes or until tender-crisp. Stir in corn and garlic and sauté for 2 minutes more. Reduce heat to low and stir in tomatoes, butter, and basil and cook until butter is just melted; season with additional salt and pepper to taste. Spoon vegetables onto serving plates and top with fish.

CHILI-GARLIC GRILLED CHICKEN WITH AVOCADO-CHERRY SALSA

Grilled chicken gets a lift with this flavor-packed marinade and fresh, fruity salsa.

ACTIVE TIME: 20 minutes
TOTAL TIME: 2 hours 40 minutes
MAKES: 4 servings

1	garlic clove, chopped
1	teaspoon chili powder
¼	cup olive oil, divided
1	tablespoon lime zest, plus 1/4 cup lime juice, divided, plus wedges for serving
	Salt and black pepper
4	(6- to 8-ounce) boneless, skinless chicken breast halves
2	cups sweet cherries, pitted and chopped
1	small shallot, chopped
½	jalapeño, seeded and chopped
¼	cup chopped fresh cilantro
1	avocado, chopped

1 Combine garlic, chili powder, 3 tablespoons oil, lime zest and 2 tablespoons juice, 1½ teaspoons salt, and ½ teaspoon pepper in a large zip-top bag. Add chicken, seal, and turn to coat. Marinate, in the refrigerator, 30 minutes and up to 2 hours.

2 Meanwhile, combine cherries, shallot, jalapeño, cilantro, remaining 1 tablespoon oil, and remaining 2 tablespoons lime juice in a bowl. Season with salt and pepper. Let stand 15 minutes. Fold in avocado.

3 Heat grill to medium-high. Remove chicken from marinade and pat dry with paper towels. Season with salt and pepper. Grill over direct heat, covered, until internal temperature reaches 165°F, 6 to 8 minutes per side. Let stand 5 minutes.

4 Serve with salsa and lime wedges.

GRILLED CUMIN-RUBBED HANGER STEAK WITH SMASHED MINTY PEAS & GRILLED BREAD

The classic steak dinner gets a fresh upgrade thanks to peas flavored with bright mint and salty Parmesan.

ACTIVE TIME: 20 minutes
TOTAL TIME: 30 minutes
MAKES: 4 servings

3	tablespoons unsalted butter, divided
1	pound fresh or frozen (thawed) peas
1	tablespoon chopped fresh mint
1	tablespoon fresh lime juice
Salt and black pepper	
1 1/2	pounds hanger steak, cut into 2 pieces
1	teaspoon ground cumin
4	slices country bread
1	tablespoon olive oil
2	ounces shaved Parmesan cheese

1 Prepare outdoor grill for direct grilling over medium-high heat. In small saucepan, melt 2 tablespoons butter over medium-high heat. Add peas and cook until soft, 6 to 8 minutes, stirring often. Add remaining 1 tablespoon butter and mash. Add mint and lime juice and stir to combine; season with salt and pepper.

2 Season steak with cumin, salt, and pepper. Grill until internal temperature reaches 130°F for medium-rare, 4 to 5 minutes per side. Let rest for 5 minutes before slicing.

3 Brush both sides of bread slices with oil. Grill until golden brown and crispy, about 1 minute per side.

4 Top pea mash with shaved Parmesan and serve alongside steak and grilled bread.

CHAPTER
THREE

a southern summer's
GREATEST
-HITS-

Burgers

Fire up the grill for one of these delicious burgers, perfect for that outdoor barbecue or summer picnic.

TEX-MEX DOUBLE BEEF BURGERS

MAKES: 4 burgers

Shape 2 pounds **ground beef chuck** into eight 4-inch patties. Season with **salt** and **black pepper**. Grill, covered, over medium-high heat until desired degree of doneness is reached, 2 to 3 minutes per side for medium. Top patties with 8 slices **extra-sharp Cheddar cheese** and grill, covered, until melted, 1 to 2 minutes. Stack 2 burgers. Serve on 4 grilled **Kaiser buns** with **pickled jalapeños**, **pico de gallo**, and **guacamole**.

TZATZIKI SALMON BURGERS

MAKES: 4 burgers

Combine 1 ½ pounds finely chopped **skinless salmon**, 1 large **egg**, ½ cup **panko bread crumbs**, 2 tablespoons chopped **capers**, 2 tablespoons chopped **fresh dill**, and 2 tablespoons **Dijon mustard**. Shape into four 4-inch patties and season with **salt** and **black pepper**. Grill, covered, over medium-high heat until cooked through, 4 to 5 minutes per side. Serve on 4 grilled **brioche rolls** with **Bibb lettuce leaves**, sliced **cucumber**, and **tzatziki**.

48

CHICKEN PARMESAN BURGERS

MAKES: 4 burgers

Combine 1 ½ pounds **ground chicken**, 1 ounce grated **Parmesan cheese**, 2 minced **garlic cloves**, and 2 tablespoons chopped **fresh oregano**. Shape into four 4-inch patties and season with **salt** and **black pepper**. Grill, covered, over medium-high heat until cooked through, 3 to 4 minutes per side. Top patties with 4 slices **fresh mozzarella** and grill, covered, until melted, 1 to 2 minutes. Serve on 4 grilled **sourdough rolls** with **mayonnaise, fresh basil,** and **tomato slices**.

SWEET & SAVORY PORK BURGERS

MAKES: 4 burgers

Combine 1 ½ pounds **ground pork** and 3 minced **scallions**; shape into four 4-inch patties. Season with **salt** and **black pepper**. Grill, covered, over medium-high heat until cooked through, 4 to 5 minutes per side. Toss 1 large **peach**, cut into wedges, with 1 teaspoon **canola oil**. Grill until warm, 1 to 2 minutes per side. Serve burgers and peaches on 4 grilled **whole wheat hamburger buns** with **arugula**, crumbled **goat cheese**, and Dijonnaise.

RANCH TURKEY BURGERS

Take a shortcut to big flavor by mixing this creamy condiment right into your burgers.

ACTIVE TIME: 20 minutes
TOTAL TIME: 1 hour
MAKES: 4 burgers

1	pound ground turkey
1	small onion, finely chopped
1	garlic clove, finely chopped
½	teaspoon salt
½	teaspoon black pepper
3	tablespoons ranch dressing
2	tablespoons vegetable oil
4	slices Swiss cheese
4	hamburger buns

1 In medium bowl, gently combine ground turkey, onion, garlic, salt, pepper, and ranch dressing. Form into four ¾-inch-thick patties. Transfer to plate, cover with plastic wrap, and chill for 30 minutes.

2 Preheat oven to 400°F. Fit wire rack over baking pan; set aside. In large skillet, heat oil over medium-high heat. Add burgers and cook until browned, about 4 minutes per side.

3 Transfer patties to baking pan, place in oven, and cook until burgers are firm and reach an internal temperature of 165°F, about 10 minutes. During last minute in oven, melt a slice of Swiss cheese over each burger. Serve on burger buns with desired toppings.

Tip

To keep your burger from getting soggy, hold off on adding the bun until you're ready to eat!

MISO-GLAZED CHICKEN BURGERS WITH CABBAGE-APPLE SLAW

A delicious alternative (saving you 109 calories and 24 grams of fat!) to beef.

TOTAL TIME: 30 minutes plus chilling
MAKES: 8 burgers

2	pounds ground white-meat chicken
1	cup whole wheat bread crumbs
1	medium onion, finely chopped (about 1 ⅓ cups)
2	celery stalks, finely chopped
2	egg whites
3	tablespoons sesame oil
2	teaspoons sea salt
2	teaspoons black pepper
½	cup miso paste
3	tablespoons brown sugar
⅓	cup plus 2 tablespoons cider vinegar
2	cups shredded cabbage (purple and/or white)
2	crisp, sweet red apples (such as Braeburn), quartered and thinly sliced
8	sesame buns, split

1 In large bowl, combine ground chicken, bread crumbs, ⅔ cup onion, celery, egg whites, and 2 tablespoons sesame oil; season with salt and pepper. Shape into 8 equal patties (about 5 ½ ounces each). Place patties between waxed paper and refrigerate at least 1 hour.

2 In small bowl, combine miso paste, 2 tablespoons brown sugar, and 2 tablespoons cider vinegar. Equally divide miso glaze into two bowls (one for grilling and 1 for drizzling on slaw). Set both aside.

3 In large bowl, toss together cabbage, apples, and remaining onion, sesame oil, brown sugar, and cider vinegar. Set aside.

4 Prepare outdoor grill for direct grilling over medium heat. Grill buns, split-side down, until warmed, about 2 minutes. Transfer to platter. Coat grill with cooking spray and grill burgers for about 6 minutes per side. Brush burgers with miso glaze from first bowl, flip, and grill for 1 ½ minutes more. Repeat for other side. Place burgers on bottom buns, then layer with slaw, a drizzle of miso glaze from second bowl, and top buns.

MINI PORTOBELLO BURGERS

Each flavorful slider also features tender grilled zucchini, squash, and eggplant. Serve with potato fries and a green salad for the perfect summer supper!

TOTAL TIME: 45 minutes
MAKES: 12 mini burgers

12	medium portobello mushrooms
2	small eggplants
2	yellow squash
2	zucchini
	Canola oil
½	teaspoon sea salt
12	mini brioche buns or dinner rolls
1 ½	teaspoons sesame oil
½	teaspoon sesame seeds
9	ounces Swiss cheese

1 Prepare outdoor grill for direct grilling, or preheat grill pan, over medium-high heat.

2 Trim stems from mushrooms. Slice eggplant, squash, and zucchini into ¼-inch-thick rounds. Brush vegetables with canola oil, sprinkle with salt, and grill until softened and grill marks have formed, about 10 minutes per side. (Brush vegetables with more oil as needed to prevent sticking.)

3 Preheat broiler on low. Transfer vegetables to baking pan. Split buns, brush tops with sesame oil, and sprinkle with sesame seeds. Layer squash, zucchini, eggplant, and 1 mushroom on bottom bun halves. Top each with cheese and broil until cheese melts, about 1 minute. Top with remaining seeded bun halves and serve hot.

CLASSIC BUTTERMILK FRIED CHICKEN

Once you've mastered this base recipe, try your hand at one of the delicious, flavor-boosting variations.

ACTIVE TIME: 1 hour
TOTAL TIME: 9 hours
MAKES: 8 servings

Salt and black pepper
2 cups buttermilk
2 large eggs
½ sweet onion, grated
2 garlic cloves, minced
5 to 6 pounds bone-in chicken parts (breasts halved, if using), skin on
4 cups self-rising flour
Canola oil, for frying
½ cup bacon drippings (optional)

1 In bowl, whisk together 5 teaspoons salt and ½ cup hot water until dissolved. Whisk in buttermilk, eggs, onion, garlic, and 1 teaspoon pepper. Add chicken and turn to coat. Cover and refrigerate, turning occasionally, for 8 hours or up to overnight.

2 Drain chicken and discard buttermilk mixture. In bowl, whisk together flour and 3 teaspoons salt. Toss chicken in flour mixture, one piece at a time, until evenly coated. Return all of chicken to flour mixture, gently toss, and let stand for 15 minutes. Toss again to make sure each piece is evenly coated. Remove, shaking off excess.

3 Preheat oven to 325°F. Line a large rimmed baking sheet with oven-safe wire rack.

4 In Dutch oven, heat 1 ½ inches oil and bacon drippings (if using) over medium-high heat to 350°F. Fry chicken, in batches, skin-side down, until golden brown, 4 to 5 minutes. Turn and fry until golden brown on second side, 4 to 5 minutes.

5 Transfer to prepared baking sheet and bake until instant-read thermometer inserted into thickest piece reads 165°F, 15 to 20 minutes. Let stand on rack for 10 minutes before serving. Serve warm, at room temperature, or chilled.

Variations

DILL PICKLE: Add ½ cup chopped **fresh dill** and ¼ cup **Dijon mustard** to buttermilk mixture. Add 1 ½ tablespoons **ground coriander** to flour mixture. Serve with **dill pickle chips.**

CHESAPEAKE: Add 3 tablespoons **lemon zest** and ⅓ cup **fresh lemon juice** to buttermilk mixture. Add 2 ½ tablespoons **Old Bay** Seasoning to flour mixture. Serve with **lemon wedges** and more Old Bay Seasoning.

3 ALARM: Add 1 (5-ounce) bottle **habanero hot sauce** and increase black pepper to 2 tablespoons in buttermilk mixture. Add 2 tablespoons **ground cayenne pepper** to flour mixture. Serve with hot sauce.

GRILLED BUFFALO CHICKEN SANDWICHES

Satisfy your wing craving with this spicy chicken sammie.

ACTIVE TIME: 25 minutes
TOTAL TIME: 40 minutes
MAKES: 4 sandwiches

1/   ⋯   sauce
1.   (½ stick) unsalted butter, melted
3   tablespoons ketchup
4   boneless skinless chicken breasts (about 1½ pounds total)
4   hamburger buns, split
½   cup ranch dressing
Blue Cheese-Apple Slaw (recipe below)

1 Prepare outdoor grill for covered direct grilling over medium-high heat.

2 In bowl, combine hot sauce, butter, and ketchup; reserve ¼ cup mixture. Add chicken to remaining mixture and toss to coat. Marinate for 20 minutes. Remove chicken from marinade; discard marinade.

3 Grill chicken, covered, until internal temperature reaches 165°F, 5 to 7 minutes per side. Grill buns until lightly toasted, 1 to 2 minutes. Spread ranch dressing on buns.

4 Serve chicken on toasted buns, topped with Blue Cheese-Apple Slaw and drizzled with reserved sauce.

★ BLUE CHEESE-APPLE SLAW

To bowl, add 1 cup packed and shredded **savoy cabbage**, 1 small sliced **apple**, 2 thinly-sliced **celery ribs**, 1½ ounces crumbled **blue cheese** (about ⅓ cup), ¼ cup coarsely chopped **fresh flat leaf parsley**, 1 thinly sliced **shallot**, 3 tablespoons **olive oil**, 1½ tablespoons **apple cider vinegar**, ½ teaspoon **granulated sugar**, and **salt** and **pepper**. Mix until well combined. ★

CURRY-LIME PORK KEBABS

Spicy curry and tangy, vibrant lime make a delicious marinade for slightly sweet and succulent pork.

TOTAL TIME: 35 minutes plus marinating
MAKES: 6 servings

¼ cup plain Greek yogurt
2 tablespoons curry powder
1 tablespoon light brown sugar
1 tablespoon soy sauce
1 tablespoon ground turmeric
1 teaspoon fresh lime juice
1 teaspoon lime zest
½ teaspoon ground coriander
½ teaspoon salt
1¼ pounds pork tenderloin, cut into 1-inch cubes
24 cherry tomatoes
12 medium cremini mushrooms, halved if necessary
6 spring onions, trimmed and halved
12 skewers
½ teaspoon black pepper
2 tablespoons chopped cilantro

1 In medium bowl, whisk together yogurt, curry powder, brown sugar, soy sauce, turmeric, lime juice and zest, coriander, and salt.

2 Place pork in 2-gallon resealable plastic bag; pour in marinade and massage to coat meat. Refrigerate for at least 1 hour or up to 6 hours.

3 Prepare outdoor grill for direct grilling over medium heat. Thread each skewer with 4 pieces pork, 2 tomatoes, 1 mushroom, and 1 onion half, alternating pork and vegetables. Spray each skewer with cooking spray and season with pepper.

4 Grill skewers until pork is cooked through, 12 to 15 minutes, turning every 4 minutes or so. Garnish cooked kebabs with cilantro.

Fries!

Don't let your burgers get lonely—serve up one of these crispy, crunchy sides to accompany your main meat!

★ SWEET POTATO FRIES

MAKES: 4 servings

Toss together 1 ½ pounds **sweet potatoes**, cut into ¼-inch-thick strips, and 2 tablespoons **canola oil**. Season with **salt** and **pepper**. Brush two large baking sheets with 3 tablespoons canola oil and heat in 450°F oven for 5 minutes. Arrange potatoes on hot pans. Bake until golden brown, 20 to 22 minutes, turning once.

★ RUSSET POTATO FRIES

MAKES: 4 servings

Toss together 1 ½ pounds **russet potatoes**, cut into ¼-inch-thick strips, and 2 tablespoons **canola oil**. Season with **salt** and **pepper**. Brush two large baking sheets with 3 tablespoons **canola oil** and heat in 450°F oven for 5 minutes. Arrange potatoes on hot pans. Bake until golden brown, 20 to 22 minutes, turning once.

★ CRISPY ZUCCHINI STRIPS

MAKES: 4 servings

Place ⅔ cup **flour** in dish. In second dish, whisk together 1 large **egg** and ⅔ cup **buttermilk**. In third dish, toss together 2 cups **panko bread crumbs** and 3 tablespoons **canola oil**. Season with **salt** and **pepper**.

Dip 3 small **zucchini**, seeds discarded and sliced into ¼-inch-thick strips, in flour, then in egg mixture, and then in bread crumb mixture.

Brush two large baking sheets with 3 tablespoons **canola oil** and heat in 450°F oven for 5 minutes. Arrange zucchini on hot pans. Bake until golden brown, 22 to 24 minutes, turning once.

★ CRISPY GREEN BEANS

MAKES: 4 servings

Place ⅔ cup **flour** in dish. In second dish, whisk together 1 large **egg** and ⅔ cup **buttermilk**. In third dish, toss together 2 cups **panko bread crumbs** and 3 tablespoons **canola oil**. Season with **salt** and **pepper**.

Dip 1 pound trimmed **green beans** in flour, then in egg mixture, and then in bread crumb mixture.

Brush two large baking sheets with 3 tablespoons **canola oil** and heat in 450°F oven for 5 minutes. Arrange green beans on hot pans. Bake until golden brown, 18 to 20 minutes, turning once.

★ ONION RINGS

MAKES: 4 servings

Place ⅔ cup **flour** in dish. In second dish, whisk together 1 large **egg** and ⅔ cup **buttermilk**. In third dish, toss together 2 cups **panko bread crumbs** and 3 tablespoons **canola oil**. Season with **salt** and **pepper**.

Dip 1 medium **sweet onion**, sliced ¼-inch thick with rings separated, in flour, then in egg mixture, and then in bread crumb mixture.

Brush two large baking sheets with 3 tablespoons **canola oil** and heat in 450°F oven for 5 minutes. Arrange onion rings on hot pans. Bake until golden brown, 16 to 18 minutes, turning once.

One-Dish Wonders!

These will quickly become your most requested sides of the summer. All recipes serve 8.

⋆ GINGER CUCUMBERS & PEPPERS

TOTAL TIME: 30 minutes

In bowl, combine ¼ cup **olive oil**, ¼ cup **rice wine vinegar**, 1 tablespoon finely grated **fresh ginger**, 2 teaspoons **granulated sugar**, and ¾ teaspoon **red pepper flakes**. Season with **salt**.

Add 2 large **cucumbers**, halved lengthwise, seeded, and sliced; ½ pound sliced **mini sweet peppers**; ½ chopped **red onion**; and ⅓ cup torn **fresh basil** and toss to combine. Chill for 15 minutes before serving.

⋆ DEVILED EGG POTATO SALAD

TOTAL TIME: 30 minutes

In medium saucepan, place 3 ½ pounds **Yukon gold potatoes**, peeled and cut into 1-inch pieces; cover with cold salted water. Simmer until tender, 4 to 5 minutes. Drain.

In bowl, combine 1 cup **mayonnaise** and 3 tablespoons **yellow mustard**. Add potatoes; 6 large **hard-boiled eggs**, peeled and chopped; 3 thinly sliced **celery ribs**, plus ¼ cup chopped **celery leaves**; 6 thinly sliced **scallions**; ⅓ cup chopped **fresh flat-leaf parsley**; and 1 (4-ounce) jar **diced pimientos**, drained, and toss to combine. Season with **salt** and **black pepper**. Garnish with **sweet paprika**.

TANGY COLLARD & CABBAGE SLAW

TOTAL TIME: 35 minutes

In bowl, combine ½ thinly sliced **red onion**, ¼ cup **cider vinegar**, 2 tablespoons **whole-grain mustard**, 1 ½ tablespoons **honey**, and ⅔ cup **olive oil**. Season with **salt** and **black pepper**. Let stand, tossing occasionally, until onion is wilted, 5 to 10 minutes.

Add 1 small bunch **collard greens** (stems discarded and leaves shredded) and ½ small head shredded **green cabbage** and toss to coat. Chill for 15 minutes. Toss in 6 slices **thick-cut bacon**, cooked and crumbled.

MOJITO WATERMELON

TOTAL TIME: 15 minutes

In bowl, whisk together 2 tablespoons **olive oil**, 2 tablespoons **lime juice**, and 1 teaspoon **granulated sugar**. Season with **salt** and **black pepper**.

Serve ½ small **watermelon** (rind discarded and sliced) topped with dressing, 2 strips **lime zest**, ⅓ cup torn **fresh mint**, and **flaky sea salt**.

5-BEAN SUMMER SALAD

This colorful salad provides a hearty, varied option that's perfect for any summer party.

TOTAL TIME: 40 minutes
MAKES: 8 servings

¼ cup olive oil
¼ cup fresh lemon juice
1 shallot, finely chopped
1 garlic clove, minced
1 tablespoon chopped fresh thyme
Salt and black pepper
1½ cups fresh lima beans
1 cup fresh black-eyed peas
½ pound smoked ham hock
1 cup fresh lady peas
½ pound yellow wax beans
½ pound sugar snap peas
½ cup chopped almonds

1 In bowl, whisk together oil, lemon juice, shallot, garlic, and thyme; season with salt and pepper.

2 In medium saucepan, add lima beans, black-eyed peas, and ham hock; cover with water. Cover and simmer until almost tender, 15 to 20 minutes. Add lady peas and simmer until peas and beans are tender, 8 to 10 minutes. Discard ham hock. Drain and run under cold water to cool.

3 In medium saucepan, cook wax beans and sugar snaps in boiling salted water until tender-crisp, 1 to 2 minutes. Drain and run under cold water to cool.

4 Add beans, peas, and almonds to dressing and toss to combine.

GRILLED POTATO SALAD WITH BACON VINAIGRETTE

The addition of delicious salty bacon transforms this summer salad from same-old to sublime.

ACTIVE TIME: 30 minutes
TOTAL TIME: 45 minutes
MAKES: 8 servings

3   pounds baby Yukon gold potatoes
Salt and black pepper
6   tablespoons olive oil, divided
6   slices center-cut bacon, cut into ½-inch pieces
2   garlic cloves, very finely chopped
¼   cup apple cider vinegar
2   tablespoons firmly packed brown sugar
8   scallions
2   tablespoons fresh marjoram, plus more for garnish

1 Prepare outdoor grill for direct grilling over medium-high heat. Line plate with paper towels.

2 In large saucepan, add potatoes and add enough cold salted water to cover by 2 inches. Cover and bring to a boil; reduce heat and simmer until easily pierced by knife, 14 to 16 minutes. Drain and let cool. Transfer to bowl and toss with 2 tablespoons oil.

3 In large skillet, cook bacon over medium heat until crisp, 5 to 7 minutes, stirring occasionally. With slotted spoon, remove to prepared plate.

4 Discard all but 1 tablespoon bacon drippings from skillet. Remove skillet from heat and add garlic, vinegar, and brown sugar to drippings, scraping up any browned bits. Whisk in remaining 4 tablespoons oil; season with salt and pepper. Transfer to bowl.

5 Grill potatoes, cut-sides down, until lightly charred, 2 to 3 minutes. Grill scallions until charred, 4 to 6 minutes, turning occasionally. Chop scallions into 1-inch pieces.

6 Add potatoes, scallions, and marjoram to bowl with dressing. Let stand for 5 minutes. Sprinkle with bacon and toss to coat. Season with salt and pepper and garnish with marjoram. Serve immediately.

Shakes!

Burgers and fries would be incomplete without the cool, creamy milk shake to finish things off.

★ BLUEBERRY-LEMON

MAKES: 2 servings

Blend 1 pint **vanilla ice cream**, 1 cup **frozen blueberries**, ⅔ cup **milk**, and 1 tablespoon each **lemon zest** and **lemon juice** until smooth. Serve topped with **fresh blueberries** and more **lemon zest**.

★ MANGO LASSIE

MAKES: 2 servings

Blend 1 pint **mango sorbet**, 1 cup **coconut milk**, ¾ cup **frozen mango chunks**, and 1 tablespoon each **lime zest** and **lime juice** until smooth. Serve topped with toasted **flaked coconut**.

★ S'MORES

MAKES: 2 servings

Blend 1 pint **rocky road ice cream** and ⅔ cup **milk** until smooth. Add ½ cup crushed **graham crackers** and pulse twice to combine. Serve topped with toasted **marshmallows**, **graham crackers**, and **chocolate sauce**.

PINEAPPLE-BOURBON

MAKES: 2 servings

Blend 1 pint **vanilla bean ice cream**, 1 cup chopped **fresh pineapple**, and 3 tablespoons **bourbon** until smooth. Drizzle **caramel sauce** inside chilled serving glasses; pour in milkshake. Serve topped with crumbled **pound cake** and 1 wedge **fresh pineapple**.

★ CHERRY MALT

MAKES: 2 servings

Blend 1 pint **cherry-vanilla ice cream**, 1 cup pitted **frozen cherries**, ⅔ cup **milk**, and 3 tablespoons **malt powder** until smooth. Serve topped with **whipped cream**, crushed **chocolate-covered malt balls**, and ★ 1 **maraschino cherry**.

CHAPTER
FOUR

get a handle on

WEEKNIGHT
—DINNERS—

PANCETTA & BRUSSELS SPROUTS LINGUINE

To add even more protein (and some plating pizazz) to this dish, top each serving with a fried egg.

TOTAL TIME: 25 minutes
MAKES: 4 servings

½	pound linguine

Salt and black pepper

6	ounces unsliced pancetta or 6 slices thick-cut bacon, diced
1	medium sweet onion, thinly sliced
1	pound Brussels sprouts, sliced
2	large garlic cloves, finely chopped
⅓	cup dry white wine
3	ounces grated Parmesan cheese (about ¾ cup), plus more, shaved, for serving

1 Cook pasta in boiling salted water according to package directions; reserve 1 cup pasta cooking water. Drain.

2 While pasta is cooking, in large deep skillet, sauté pancetta and onion over medium heat until pancetta is browned and onions are caramelized, 8 to 10 minutes, stirring occasionally. Add Brussels sprouts and garlic and sauté until leaves are bright green, 2 minutes, stirring. Stir in wine, scraping brown bits from bottom of skillet. Add pasta, grated Parmesan, and ½ to ¾ cup reserved pasta water and stir until Parmesan is melted and pasta is creamy and well coated. Season with salt and pepper.

3 Serve immediately sprinkled with pepper and shaved Parmesan.

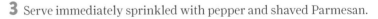

PASTA WITH SAUTÉED PEPPERS, ZUCCHINI & SMOKED MOZZARELLA

This fresh pasta dish brings a veggie twist to the traditional spaghetti night.

ACTIVE TIME: 10 minutes
TOTAL TIME: 30 minutes
MAKES: 4 servings

2	tablespoons unsalted butter
1	tablespoon olive oil
3	small bell peppers, thinly sliced
1	small onion, thinly sliced
	Salt and black pepper
2	medium zucchini, cut into ½-inch-thick slices
12	ounces fettuccine or tagliatelle pasta
4	ounces smoked mozzarella, grated (about 1 cup), plus more for serving
¼	cup fresh torn basil, plus more for serving

1 In large skillet, heat butter and oil over medium-high heat. Add peppers and onion; season with salt and pepper. Cook until almost tender, 10 to 12 minutes, stirring often. Add zucchini and cook until peppers are tender and zucchini is tender-crisp, 4 to 6 minutes.

2 Cook pasta according to package directions. Reserve 1 cup pasta cooking water; drain.

3 Add pasta, mozzarella, basil, and ½ cup reserved pasta water to pepper mixture and toss to coat. (Add more pasta water, if needed, to create a sauce.) Season with salt and pepper.

4 Serve topped with mozzarella and basil.

CREAMY CHICKEN & BROCCOLI-PESTO BOW TIES

Toasted pecans add unexpected warmth and crunch to this creamy pasta dish.

TOTAL TIME: 20 minutes
MAKES: 4 servings

2   cups broccoli florets
Salt and black pepper
½   pound farfalle (bow tie) pasta
1   small bunch fresh basil (1 ounce), stems removed
2   garlic cloves
¼   cup olive oil
2   teaspoons lemon zest, plus more for serving
¼   teaspoon red pepper flakes
3   ounces grated Parmesan cheese (about ¾ cup)
4   ounces mascarpone or cream cheese, at room temperature
2   cups shredded rotisserie chicken, warmed
⅓   cup chopped toasted pecans (optional)

1 Cook broccoli in boiling salted water until tender, 5 minutes. With slotted spoon, remove to bowl. Add pasta to same cooking water and cook according to package directions; drain.

2 In food processor with knife blade attached, process basil, garlic, oil, lemon zest, red pepper, and Parmesan until finely chopped. Add broccoli and pulse until coarsely chopped, 4 to 6 times; season with salt and pepper.

3 Stir broccoli pesto and mascarpone into pasta until well coated; fold in chicken.

4 Serve sprinkled with lemon zest and pecans, if desired.

CHARD & FETA-STUFFED ACORN SQUASH

This hearty stuffed squash is super low-maintenance and extremely filling. For photo, see page 5.

ACTIVE TIME: 25 minutes
TOTAL TIME: 1 hour 15 minutes
MAKES: 4 servings

2   acorn squash, halved crosswise and seeded
1 ½   tablespoons olive oil, plus more for skillet
1   large leek (white and light green parts only), halved and sliced
1   bunch Swiss chard, chopped
2   garlic cloves, chopped
1   cup fresh bread crumbs
¼   cup raisins
3   tablespoons pine nuts
2   ounces feta cheese, crumbled (about ½ cup)
Salt and black pepper

1 Preheat oven to 400°F. Grease 12-inch cast-iron skillet. Place squash, cut-sides down, in prepared skillet. Cover with foil and bake until tender, 34 to 36 minutes. Remove to plate.

2 In same skillet, heat oil over medium heat. Add leeks and cook until tender, 2 to 4 minutes, stirring occasionally. Stir in chard and garlic and cook until wilted, 2 to 3 minutes, stirring. Stir in bread crumbs, raisins, pine nuts, and feta; season with salt and pepper.

3 Fill squash with chard mixture, dividing evenly. Place squash, cut-sides up, in skillet and return to oven. Bake until tops are golden brown, 15 to 20 minutes.

BAKED JAMBALAYA

Bake up this spiced Cajun recipe in no time at all.

ACTIVE TIME: 25 minutes
TOTAL TIME: 1 hour 25 minutes
MAKES: 6 servings

2	tablespoons canola oil
1	medium onion, chopped
1	green bell pepper, chopped
1	celery rib, sliced
8	ounces smoked Andouille sausage, chopped
1 1/2	cups jasmine rice
2	cups chicken stock
1	can (14 1/2 ounces) diced tomatoes
1 1/2	teaspoons Creole seasoning
1	bay leaf

Salt and black pepper

1	pound medium shrimp, peeled and deveined
1/4	cup chopped fresh flat-leaf parsley
2	scallions, sliced

Hot sauce, for serving

1 Preheat oven to 325°F. In 12-inch cast-iron skillet, heat oil over medium-high heat. Add onion, pepper, celery, and sausage and cook until lightly browned, 8 to 10 minutes, stirring often. Stir in rice and cook for 1 minute. Remove from heat and stir in stock, tomatoes, Creole seasoning, and bay leaf; season with salt and pepper. Cover with foil.

2 Bake until rice is tender, 45 to 50 minutes. Remove from oven, uncover, and gently stir in shrimp and parsley. Re-cover and bake just until shrimp are opaque throughout, 5 to 7 minutes.

3 Serve topped with scallions and hot sauce alongside.

STEAKHOUSE STEAKS WITH CREAMY KALE

This one-dish dinner makes evening cooking a breeze.

ACTIVE TIME: 30 minutes
TOTAL TIME: 55 minutes
MAKES: 4 servings

2   strip steaks (each ¾- to 1-inch thick)
1   tablespoon Montreal steak seasoning
Salt
2   teaspoons canola oil
1   small onion, chopped
2   bunches curly kale, stems discarded and leaves chopped
2   garlic cloves, minced
3   ounces cream cheese, cut up
½   cup half-and-half
2   teaspoons fresh lemon juice
⅛ to ¼ teaspoon red pepper flakes
Toasted bread, for serving

1 Let steaks stand at room temperature for 20 minutes; season with steak seasoning and salt.

2 In 12-inch cast-iron skillet, heat oil over medium-high heat. Add steaks and cook until internal temperature reaches 130°F (for medium-rare), 4 to 5 minutes per side. Remove to cutting board and allow to rest for 5 minutes before slicing.

3 To same skillet, add onion and cook until tender, 2 to 4 minutes, stirring. Add kale (in batches) and garlic and cook until kale is just wilted, 4 to 6 minutes, stirring. Reduce heat to low and stir in cream cheese and half-and-half until melted and creamy. Stir in lemon juice and pepper flakes; season with salt.

4 Serve steak with creamy kale and toasted bread.

Country Know-How

Keep your cast-iron skillet simmering for years to come with these simple rules for cleaning in between seasonings.

1 Wash with water after each use. Yes, you can—and should—wash cast iron.

2 Remove unwanted leftovers with a mild abrasive, such as Bonami®.

3 To dry, place on the stove over low heat for 1 to 2 minutes.

4 Line with paper towels before storing.

HERB-GARLIC CRUSTED FLANK STEAK WITH PAN-ROASTED GRAPES

This quick and easy flank steak dinner can be on the table in less than 30 minutes.

TOTAL TIME: 28 minutes
MAKES: 4 servings

2   teaspoons chopped fresh thyme
2   teaspoons chopped fresh rosemary
1   large garlic clove, minced
1 ½ teaspoons salt
¾   teaspoon black pepper
1   flank steak (1 ½ pounds)
2   tablespoons olive oil, divided
3   cups assorted grapes, halved and whole
2   shallots, chopped
1 to 2 tablespoons white balsamic vinegar
½   cup freshly crumbled blue cheese
Mashed potatoes, for serving

1 In small bowl, combine thyme, rosemary, garlic, salt, and pepper; rub mixture all over steak. In large, heavy skillet, heat 1 tablespoon oil over medium-high heat. Add steak and cook for 6 to 7 minutes per side or until desired degree of doneness is reached. Remove and cover loosely with foil.

2 Reduce heat to medium. Add remaining 1 tablespoon oil to pan and sauté grapes and shallots until grapes just begin to soften, 5 to 6 minutes. Remove from heat and let stand for 1 minute. Stir in vinegar and season with salt and pepper, to taste.

3 Slice steak against the grain into thin slices. Arrange on serving platter, spooning grapes and cheese over meat. Sprinkle with additional fresh herbs, if desired. Serve with mashed potatoes.

PORK LOIN WITH BRAISED ROSEMARY WHITE BEANS

The smoky, tender pork pairs perfectly with the fragrant, herbed white beans. For photo, see page 4.

ACTIVE TIME: 30 minutes
TOTAL TIME: 1 hour
MAKES: 4 to 6 servings

1   boneless pork loin (1 1/2 to 2 pounds)
1   tablespoon chopped fresh thyme
Salt and black pepper
2   tablespoons olive oil
1   medium onion, chopped
3   garlic cloves, chopped
1/4 cup dry white wine
2   cans (15 1/2 ounces each) cannellini beans
1 1/2 cups chicken stock
1/2 cup sliced sundried tomatoes ·
1   tablespoon chopped fresh rosemary, plus sprigs for serving

1 Preheat oven to 400°F. Rub pork with thyme; season with salt and pepper. In 12-inch cast-iron skillet, heat oil over medium-high heat. Add pork and cook until browned on all sides, 6 to 8 minutes. Remove to plate.

2 To same skillet, add onion and garlic and cook until golden, 4 to 6 minutes, stirring occasionally. Stir in wine, scraping up brown bits from bottom of skillet. Stir in beans, stock, tomatoes, and rosemary. Place pork on top of bean mixture.

3 Bake until instant-read thermometer inserted into thickest part of pork registers 145°F, 18 to 20 minutes. Let rest, loosely covered with foil, for 10 minutes before slicing.

4 Serve garnished with rosemary sprigs.

HOISIN-GLAZED PORK TENDERLOIN WITH ASIAN RICE SALAD

This sweet-and-spicy Asian-inspired meal hits all the right flavor notes.

ACTIVE TIME: 15 minutes
TOTAL TIME: 40 minutes
MAKES: 4 servings

2   pork tenderloins (1 ½ pounds total)
Salt and black pepper
½   cup hoisin sauce
1   cup jasmine rice
2   tablespoons Ponzu (see Tip)
1   tablespoon fresh lime juice
1   teaspoon toasted sesame oil
1   Persian cucumber, thinly sliced
3   ounces wax beans, sliced on the bias
¼   cup roasted peanuts, chopped
½   cup fresh cilantro, torn
1   tablespoon toasted sesame seeds, plus more for serving
1   small red chile, thinly sliced

1 Preheat oven to 425°F. Line large baking sheet with aluminum foil.

2 Place pork on prepared baking sheet and season with salt and pepper. Brush pork on all sides with hoisin. Place in oven and roast until instant-read thermometer inserted in thickest part registers 145°F, 15 to 25 minutes. Let rest for 5 minutes before slicing.

3 Meanwhile, cook rice according to package directions; cool slightly. In bowl, whisk together Ponzu, lime juice, and sesame oil. Add cucumber, beans, peanuts, cilantro, sesame seeds, chile, and rice and toss to combine; season with salt and pepper.

4 Serve sliced pork over rice and garnished with sesame seeds.

Tip

Ponzu is a thin, citrus-based sauce often used in Asian cuisine. It's available in the Asian section of the grocery store.

CHIPOTLE CHICKEN FAJITAS

These spicy chicken fajitas take barely any time and require only a cast-iron skillet. Oh, and they're great, too!

TOTAL TIME: 30 minutes
MAKES: 4 servings

1	pound boneless skinless chicken breasts, cut into thin strips
1	teaspoon ground cumin
1	teaspoon chili powder

Salt and black pepper

1	tablespoon canola oil
1	red bell pepper, sliced
1	small onion, sliced
1	cup sliced mushrooms
3	garlic cloves, chopped
1	tablespoon chopped chipotles in adobo
1 ½	tablespoons fresh lime juice
8	flour tortillas, warmed

Grated Cheddar cheese, cilantro, and lime wedges, for serving

1 Season chicken with cumin, chili powder, salt, and pepper. In 12-inch cast-iron skillet, heat oil over medium heat. Add chicken and cook until cooked through, 5 to 7 minutes, stirring occasionally. Remove to plate.

2 To same skillet, add pepper, onion, mushrooms, and garlic and cook until soft, 4 to 6 minutes, stirring occasionally. Stir in chipotles, lime juice, and chicken. Cook until warm; season with salt and pepper.

3 Serve chicken and vegetables with tortillas and toppings.

CRISPY CHICKEN THIGHS WITH PEPPERS & SALSA VERDE

Crispy, juicy chicken joins forces with colorful peppers and a bright salsa in this quick and hearty weeknight dish. For photo, see page 66.

TOTAL TIME: 20 minutes
MAKES: 4 servings

1 1/4 cups low-sodium chicken broth

1 box (5.8 ounces) roasted garlic and olive oil couscous

2 teaspoons vegetable oil

6 large bone-in chicken thighs, trimmed with skin on (about 2 3/4 pounds total)

1 1/2 teaspoons salt

3/4 teaspoon black pepper

3 medium colorful bell peppers (any colors), cut into 1/2-inch thick strips

1/2 medium sweet onion, sliced

2 garlic cloves, thinly sliced

Caper Salsa Verde (recipe below)

1 Preheat oven to 425°F. In 12-inch cast-iron skillet, bring broth to a boil. Pour over couscous in medium bowl; cover and set aside.

2 In same skillet, heat oil over medium-high heat until very hot. Sprinkle chicken with salt and pepper and place in skillet, skin-side down, and cook for 10 minutes or until skin is browned and crispy. Turn chicken over and cook for 4 minutes longer. Transfer to a plate; discard drippings.

3 Add peppers, onion, and garlic to skillet and sauté for 3 minutes. Arrange chicken on top of peppers, skin-side up. Place skillet in oven and bake for 10 minutes or until done.

4 Fluff couscous with fork. Serve chicken and peppers on couscous and top with desired amount of salsa.

★ CAPER SALSA VERDE

In bowl, stir together 1/4 cup chopped **fresh parsley**, 1/4 cup chopped **fresh basil**, 1 finely chopped **green onion**, 1/4 cup **extra-virgin olive oil**, 2 tablespoons coarsely chopped **capers**, and 1 1/2 tablespoons **fresh lemon juice**; season with **salt** and **pepper**, to taste.

BAKED COCONUT TENDERS WITH STRAWBERRY-MANGO SALSA

Tender and oven-fried, these chicken tenders get a hint of sweetness from their crispy coconut crust and tangy fruit salsa side.

ACTIVE TIME: 20 minutes
TOTAL TIME: 36 minutes
MAKES: 4 servings

3   boneless skinless chicken breasts (about 1 pound total)
Salt and black pepper
½   cup cornstarch
1½ teaspoons garlic powder
2   large eggs, beaten
1   cup sweetened flaked coconut
1   cup panko bread crumbs
1   teaspoon paprika
Strawberry-Mango Salsa (recipe below)
Lime wedges, for serving

★ STRAWBERRY-MANGO SALSA

In bowl, combine ¾ cup finely chopped **fresh strawberries**, ¾ cup finely chopped **fresh mango**, ½ cup finely chopped small **shallot**, 2 tablespoons chopped **fresh cilantro**, 1 tablespoon **hot pepper jelly**, 1 tablespoon **fresh lime juice**, and **salt** and **pepper**. Let stand for 10 minutes before serving.

1 Preheat oven to 425°F. Set ovenproof wire rack on rimmed baking sheet and spray with cooking spray.

2 Cut chicken into ½- to ¾-inch-thick strips; season with salt and pepper. In shallow dish, stir together cornstarch and garlic. In second shallow dish, add egg. In third shallow dish, stir together coconut, bread crumbs, paprika, and ½ teaspoon each salt and pepper.

3 Working one piece at a time, dip chicken in cornstarch mixture, then in egg mixture, and then in coconut mixture, pressing gently to help adhere. Transfer to greased rack. Spray chicken with cooking spray until well coated.

4 Bake until golden brown and cooked through, 16 to 20 minutes. Serve with Strawberry-Mango Salsa and lime wedges.

CHAPTER FIVE

- bring back -

SUNDAY SUPPERS

PORK TAMALE PIE

The gentle heat from the oven thickens the sauce and slowly cooks the pork into tender shreds in this fix-it-and-forget-it dish. For a little extra kick, sub pepper Jack for the Cheddar in the cornbread crust.

ACTIVE TIME: 15 minutes
TOTAL TIME: 4 hours 45 minutes
MAKES: 4 to 6 servings

2   cans (14 ½ ounces each) stewed tomatoes
1   small onion, chopped
1   poblano pepper, chopped
2   garlic cloves, chopped
2   teaspoons chili powder
1   teaspoon dried oregano
¾   teaspoon ground cumin
Salt and black pepper
1 ½ pounds boneless pork shoulder, excess fat removed
½   teaspoon granulated sugar
Cheddar-Cilantro Cornbread Crust (recipe at right)

1 Preheat oven to 325°F. Spray 2-quart baking dish with cooking spray.

2 In bowl, combine tomatoes, onion, pepper, garlic, chili powder, oregano, cumin, and ¼ teaspoon each salt and pepper; transfer to prepared baking dish. Rub pork with sugar, 1 teaspoon salt, and ½ teaspoon pepper; place on top of tomato mixture.

3 Bake, uncovered, until pork is fork-tender, 3 ½ to 4 hours. With two forks, shred pork into bite-size pieces; stir back into dish with sauce.

4 Increase oven temperature to 425°F. Spread Cheddar-Cilantro Cornbread Crust over pork mixture, leaving 1-inch border all around. Bake until golden brown and crust is set, 18 to 20 minutes. Let stand for 10 minutes before serving.

★ CHEDDAR-CILANTRO CORNBREAD CRUST

In bowl, combine ⅓ cup **yellow cornmeal**, 3 tablespoons **all-purpose flour**, ¾ teaspoon **baking powder**, and ¼ teaspoon **salt**. Stir in 2 ounces shredded **extra-sharp Cheddar cheese** (about ½ cup) and 2 tablespoons chopped **fresh cilantro**. In second bowl, whisk together ¼ cup **buttermilk**, 1 large **egg**, and 1 tablespoon melted **unsalted butter**; add to cornmeal mixture and stir just until dry ingredients are moistened.

RED-EYE BRISKET STEW

This hearty classic gets a zesty kick from a combination of coffee, Dijon mustard, and pickled red onions.

ACTIVE TIME: 25 minutes
TOTAL TIME: 8 hours 25 minutes
MAKES: 4 to 6 servings

2 ½ cups beef stock
3 tablespoons all-purpose flour
1 tablespoon Dijon mustard
Salt and black pepper
1 tablespoon canola oil
2 ½ pounds brisket, trimmed and cut into 2-inch pieces
¾ cup brewed coffee
1 ½ pounds new potatoes, halved
½ pound carrots, cut into 2-inch pieces
½ pound parsnips, cut into 2-inch pieces
1 onion, chopped
4 garlic cloves, chopped
4 fresh thyme sprigs, plus leaves for garnish
1 bay leaf
Pickled Red Onions (recipe at left)
Cornbread, for serving

PICKLED RED ONIONS

In medium saucepan, stir together 1 cup **seasoned rice vinegar**, 1 chopped **garlic clove**, ½ cup **water**, and 2 teaspoons **salt**. Bring to a simmer over medium heat. Remove from heat and stir in ½ sliced **red onion**. Let stand until softened, 25 to 30 minutes.

1 In 6-quart slow-cooker bowl, whisk together stock, flour, mustard, 1 teaspoon salt, and ½ teaspoon pepper.

2 In large skillet, heat oil over medium-high heat. Season brisket with salt and pepper. Cook, in batches, until browned on all sides, 4 to 6 minutes. Remove to slow cooker. To same skillet, add coffee and cook, scraping up browned bits, for 30 seconds; add to slow cooker.

3 Add potatoes, carrots, parsnips, onion, garlic, thyme, and bay leaf to slow cooker and stir to combine. Cover and cook until beef is tender, on low for 7 to 8 hours or on high for 3 to 4 hours. Discard thyme sprigs and bay leaf; season with salt and pepper.

4 Serve topped with thyme leaves and Pickled Red Onions, and cornbread alongside.

SPINACH & PINE NUT–STUFFED LEG OF LAMB

Sweet golden raisins and buttery pine nuts perfectly complement this flavorful roast leg of lamb.

ACTIVE TIME: 20 minutes
TOTAL TIME: 1 hour 30 minutes
MAKES: 8 servings

3	tablespoons olive oil
1	large yellow onion, chopped
1	package (5 ounces) baby spinach
2	garlic cloves
½	cup pine nuts
½	cup golden raisins
1	boneless leg of lamb, butterflied (5 pounds)
1	tablespoon salt
1	teaspoon black pepper
1	teaspoon sweet paprika
1	teaspoon ground coriander

1 Preheat oven to 400°F. In large sauté pan, heat oil over medium-high heat. Add onion and sauté until softened, 8 minutes. Add spinach and garlic and sauté until spinach is wilted, 4 minutes. Remove pan from heat and stir in pine nuts and raisins.

2 Sprinkle lamb with ½ tablespoon salt and ½ teaspoon pepper; flip meat and repeat. Sprinkle one side with paprika and coriander, and then evenly spread spinach mixture on same side. Roll up from one long side and tie with kitchen twine every 2 inches.

3 Transfer lamb to roasting pan and roast until instant-read thermometer reaches 140°F when inserted into center (for medium-rare), about 1 hour. Remove from oven and let rest for 10 minutes before removing twine and slicing meat.

FLATTENED CHICKEN & GRILLED ROMAINE WITH PARSLEY-LEMON SAUCE

This grilled chicken deserves a permanent spot in your Sunday supper lineup. For photo, see page 86.

ACTIVE TIME: 15 minutes
TOTAL TIME: 55 minutes
MAKES: 4 servings

1	chicken (2 ½ to 3 pounds), backbone removed and chicken flattened (see Tip)
4	garlic cloves, chopped

Salt and black pepper

1	ounce grated Parmesan cheese (about ¼ cup)
¼	cup chopped fresh flat-leaf parsley
¼	cup toasted hazelnuts or almonds, chopped
1	teaspoon lemon zest, plus 2 tablespoons lemon juice
4	tablespoons olive oil, divided
2	romaine hearts, halved lengthwise

1 Prepare outdoor grill for covered direct and indirect grilling over medium-high heat.

2 Loosen skin of chicken and spread garlic underneath; season with salt and pepper. Cover and grill over direct heat, breast-side down until golden brown and charred, 5 to 7 minutes. Flip and grill over indirect heat, covered, until instant-read thermometer inserted into thickest part registers 165°F, 35 to 40 minutes.

3 Meanwhile, in bowl, combine Parmesan, parsley, hazelnuts, lemon zest and juice, and 3 tablespoons oil; season with salt and pepper.

4 Brush romaine with remaining 1 tablespoon oil; season with salt and pepper. Grill over direct heat, turning once, until charred and wilted, 1 to 3 minutes.

5 Serve chicken and romaine topped with parsley-lemon sauce.

Tip

To remove a chicken's backbone, insert kitchen shears in cavity and cut entire length on one side of the backbone. Rotate the chicken 180 degrees, and then cut along the other side.

SLOW-COOKER MEATBALLS

This versatile Italian favorite has never been easier to make. For a fun twist, make mini meatball sliders with toasted dinner rolls, provolone, and sliced sweet-hot banana peppers. For photo, see page 1.

ACTIVE TIME: 30 minutes
TOTAL TIME: 9 hours 30 minutes
MAKES: 12 servings (36 meatballs)

½   cup panko bread crumbs
2   ounces grated Parmesan cheese (about ½ cup)
⅓   cup chopped fresh flat-leaf parsley leaves
⅓   cup milk
1   large egg
7   large garlic cloves, finely chopped and divided
2   pounds lean (85%) ground beef
½   pound Italian sausage, casings removed
Canola oil, for baking sheet
1   medium sweet onion, finely chopped
2   tablespoons olive oil
2   teaspoons Italian seasoning
¼   teaspoon red pepper flakes
1   can (28 ounces) crushed tomatoes
1   can (28 ounces) diced tomatoes
1   can (28 ounces) tomato sauce
2   teaspoons granulated sugar
1   small bunch fresh basil, finely chopped

1 Preheat oven to 425°F. In bowl, combine panko, Parmesan, parsley, milk, egg, and 3 garlic cloves; let stand for 10 minutes. Add ground beef and sausage and gently combine using your hands. Shape into 36 (1- to 1½-inch) balls. Line rimmed baking sheet with foil and lightly grease with canola oil. Place meatballs on prepared baking sheet and bake until browned, 15 minutes. Drain well.

2 In microwave-safe bowl, combine onion, olive oil, Italian seasoning, and red pepper. Microwave, stirring once, until onion is tender, 3 to 4 minutes. In 6-quart slow-cooker bowl, combine onion mixture, crushed tomatoes, diced tomatoes, tomato sauce, and sugar. Gently stir meatballs into sauce. Cover and cook on low until the flavors are combined, 8 to 9 hours. Stir in basil.

SWISS CHARD & LAMB BAKE

Don't worry if the phyllo wrinkles and buckles when layering—the texture gives the finished dish an elegant look.

ACTIVE TIME: 35 minutes
TOTAL TIME: 1 hour 30 minutes
MAKES: 4 to 6 servings

2	teaspoons olive oil
1	medium onion, chopped
½	pound ground lamb
3	garlic cloves, chopped
1	can (14 ounces) artichoke hearts, drained, squeezed dry, and chopped
2	bunches Swiss chard (about 1 pound total), trimmed with stems and leaves chopped
¼	cup chopped fresh flat-leaf parsley
1	tablespoon chopped fresh dill
4	ounces feta cheese, crumbled (about 1 cup)
2	large eggs
½	teaspoon salt
¼	teaspoon black pepper
7	sheets (each 18" by 14") frozen phyllo dough, thawed
3	tablespoons unsalted butter, melted

1 Preheat oven to 375°F. Spray 2-quart baking dish with cooking spray.

2 In large saucepan, heat oil over medium-high heat. Add onion and lamb and cook, breaking up meat with back of spoon, until lamb is browned, 8 to 10 minutes. Add garlic and artichokes and cook until heated through, 1 to 2 minutes, stirring occasionally. Stir in chard and cook until wilted, 4 to 6 minutes, stirring occasionally.

3 Remove from heat and stir in parsley and dill. Cool for 10 minutes. Stir in cheese, eggs, salt, and pepper. Transfer mixture to prepared baking dish.

4 If needed, trim phyllo so it overhangs the baking dish by 1 inch on all sides. Place one sheet on filling, allowing edges to hang over side of dish; brush very lightly with butter. Repeat with remaining phyllo sheets and butter.

5 Bake until golden brown, 30 to 35 minutes. Let stand for 10 minutes before serving.

Freezing a Casserole

A frozen casserole will keep for 3 months (any longer and you'll risk freezer burn). Before assembling, line the baking dish with a large piece of greased aluminum foil. Prepare the casserole as instructed (not including the topping); freeze. Once frozen, lift from the dish and wrap with the excess foil. Label, wrap in plastic wrap, and return to the freezer.

Ready to bake? Unwrap and place the frozen block in a dish. Thaw overnight in the refrigerator, add toppings, and bake as instructed.

COWBOY BRISKET

Every country home needs something simmering in the kitchen, so fire up this versatile big-batch recipe. Then choose one of five delicious dinner options!

ACTIVE TIME: 15 minutes
TOTAL TIME: 8 hours 10 minutes
MAKES: 15 servings

2   tablespoons cowboy rub (such as McCormick® Grill Mates®)
1   tablespoon dark brown sugar
2   teaspoons smoked paprika
1½ teaspoons salt
1   teaspoon ground cumin
1   flat-cut brisket (6 pounds)
1   large sweet onion, sliced
3   garlic cloves, minced
1   cup chopped fresh cilantro

In bowl, stir together cowboy rub, sugar, paprika, salt, and cumin. Trim fat from brisket, leaving a thin layer; cut into 3-inch chunks. Rub brisket pieces evenly with spice mixture. In lightly greased 5- to 6-quart slow-cooker bowl, add onions and garlic; arrange meat on top and sprinkle with cilantro. Cover and cook on low for 8 to 9 hours or until brisket pieces shred easily with a fork. Serve drizzled with small amount of cooking liquid, or cover and chill for up to 4 days.

Variations

TACOS: Try brisket on warmed **tortillas** with your favorite toppings, such as **pico de gallo**, crumbled **queso fresco**, and **lime wedges**.

OPEN-FACE SANDWICHES: Toss shredded **cabbage**, grated **carrots**, and diced **cucumbers** with **ranch dressing** and a squeeze of **lime juice**. Pile brisket on large squares of toasted **cornbread** and top with the slaw and sliced **green onions**.

PIZZA: Spread **pizza dough** with **barbecue sauce**. Sprinkle with brisket, shredded **pepper Jack cheese**, diced **red onion**, and **red bell peppers**. Bake according to dough directions, sprinkling with **cilantro** just before serving.

BAKED SWEET POTATOES: Wilt **spinach** in **garlic butter**. Split roasted **sweet potatoes**; fill each with brisket and buttered spinach. Dollop with **sour cream** and sprinkle with chopped **bacon** and diced **red onion**.

RAVIOLI: Toss brisket with hot cooked **cheese ravioli**, fresh **arugula**, chopped **fresh parsley**, and halved **grape tomatoes**. Sprinkle with grated **Parmesan cheese**.

MEATBALL & SPINACH BAKED ZITI

Loaded with cheese, pasta, and tender meatballs, this bake guarantees that every plate with be wiped clean.

ACTIVE TIME: 25 minutes
TOTAL TIME: 1 hour
MAKES: 4 to 6 servings

2	cups ziti pasta
1	teaspoon salt
½	teaspoon black pepper
1	pound ground round
½	small onion, chopped
¼	cup panko bread crumbs
2	garlic cloves, chopped
1	large egg
1	tablespoon canola oil
¼	cup dry red wine
1	jar (24 ounces) marinara sauce
2	bunches flat-leaf spinach, stems discarded and leaves torn (about 4 cups)
3	tablespoons chopped fresh flat-leaf parsley, plus more for garnish
3	tablespoons chopped fresh basil, plus more for garnish
8	ounces bocconcini (small fresh mozzarella balls)

1 Preheat oven to 350°F. Spray 2-quart baking dish with cooking spray.

2 In large pot of boiling salted water, cook pasta until al dente. In bowl, gently combine ground round, onion, bread crumbs, garlic, egg, salt, and pepper; shape into 16 meatballs.

3 In large skillet, heat oil over medium heat. Add meatballs and cook until brown on all sides, 6 to 8 minutes, turning occasionally. Stir in wine, gently scraping up brown bits from bottom of skillet. Stir in marinara, spinach, parsley, and basil and bring to a simmer. Remove from heat and fold in cooked pasta.

4 Transfer mixture to prepared baking dish; top with bocconcini. Bake until cheese is melted and edges are bubbly, 25 to 30 minutes. Let stand for 10 minutes before serving. Garnish with parsley and basil.

Tip

Be sure to drain the pasta while it's still firm in the center. It will soften when baking while also soaking up the delicious flavors from the sauce.

ROASTED CHICKEN & WINTER SQUASH

While certainly company-worthy, this roast chicken is low-key and simple to prepare. Serve it with the Winter Chopped Salad (see recipe, opposite) for a perfect weekend meal.

ACTIVE TIME: 20 minutes
TOTAL TIME: 1 hour 30 minutes
MAKES: 8 servings

3	delicata squash, halved, seeded, and sliced ¾-inch thick
3	celery ribs, cut into 3-inch pieces
1	large red onion, cut into wedges
2	heads garlic, cut in half crosswise
1	bunch fresh thyme (about 20 sprigs)
2	tablespoons olive oil

Salt and black pepper

2	whole chickens (3 ½ to 4 pounds each), giblets discarded
2	lemons, halved

1 Preheat oven to 425°F. In roasting pan, toss together squash, celery, onion, garlic, oil, and half of thyme sprigs; season with salt and pepper. Arrange in even layer.

2 Season chickens (including cavities) with 5 teaspoons salt and 2 teaspoons pepper. Stuff cavities with lemons and remaining half of thyme sprigs. Tie legs with kitchen twine and tuck wing tips under. Place on top of squash mixture.

3 Roast until the internal temperature reaches 165°F, 1 hour to 1 hour 10 minutes.

4 Remove chickens and vegetables to platter; let rest for 10 minutes before carving chickens. Reserve ¾ cup pan drippings for Pan-Drippings Vinaigrette (see recipe, opposite).

WINTER CHOPPED SALAD

This salad is loaded with delicious golden beets,
a good source of folate, manganese, and potassium.

ACTIVE TIME: 25 minutes
TOTAL TIME: 1 hour
MAKES: 8 servings

1 pound medium golden beets
½ loaf sourdough bread, torn into bite-size pieces
2 tablespoons olive oil
Salt and black pepper
3 romaine hearts, chopped
¼ small head red cabbage, shredded
½ head cauliflower, finely chopped
½ English cucumber, sliced
¼ cup roasted salted sunflower seeds
Pan-Drippings Vinaigrette (recipe at right)

1 Preheat oven to 425°F. Wrap beets in large piece of foil and bake until easily pierced with paring knife, 35 to 45 minutes. When cool, peel and cut into wedges.

2 On baking sheet, toss together bread and oil; arrange in single layer and season with salt and pepper. Bake until golden brown, 8 to 10 minutes.

3 In bowl, toss together romaine, cabbage, cauliflower, cucumbers, sunflower seeds, beets, toasted bread, and ½ cup Pan-Drippings Vinaigrette; season with salt and pepper. Serve with remaining vinaigrette alongside.

★ PAN-DRIPPINGS VINAIGRETTE

In bowl, whisk together 2 tablespoons **red wine vinegar** and 1 minced **shallot**; let stand for 10 minutes. Whisk in ¾ cup **reserved pan drippings** (from Roasted Chicken & Winter Squash, recipe opposite), 2 tablespoons chopped **fresh chives**, 1 ½ teaspoons **Dijon mustard**, and pinch **granulated sugar**; season with **salt** and **pepper**.

HAM & LEEK BAKED GNOCCHI

Whip up this fun twist on mac 'n' cheese when you're in the mood for something warm and hearty. Kids will love it, too!

ACTIVE TIME: 10 minutes
TOTAL TIME: 55 minutes
MAKES: 4 servings

1   package (16 ounces) gnocchi
6   ounces fontina cheese, shredded (about 1 ½ cups)
½   cup finely chopped ham
1 ¼ cups whole milk
3   tablespoons all-purpose flour
1   garlic clove, chopped
½   teaspoon black pepper
2   slices sandwich bread, torn
2   tablespoons unsalted butter, melted
1   leek, sliced and rings separated
Sliced fresh chives, for garnish

1 Preheat oven to 350°F. Spray four 10-ounce ramekins with cooking spray; place on baking sheet.

2 In bowl, combine gnocchi, cheese, and ham. Transfer to prepared ramekins, dividing evenly. Whisk together milk, flour, garlic, and pepper until flour is dissolved, 30 seconds. Pour over gnocchi, dividing evenly.

3 In bowl, stir together bread and butter until coated; toss in leeks. Sprinkle over gnocchi, dividing evenly. Bake until golden brown and bubbly, 34 to 36 minutes. Let stand for 5 minutes before serving. Garnish with chives.

CHAPTER
SIX

- the -
SWEETEST
- THINGS -

STRAWBERRY-LIMEADE CAKE WITH STRAWBERRY–CREAM CHEESE FROSTING

This dessert is every bit as fruity and fresh as its beverage namesake. For a pretty presentation, turn a porcelain quiche dish upside down to serve as a quick cake display.

ACTIVE TIME: 45 minutes
TOTAL TIME: 5 hours 30 minutes
MAKES: 12 to 15 servings

★ **STRAWBERRY-CREAM CHEESE FROSTING**

With an electric mixer set on medium speed, beat 12 ounces room-temperature **cream cheese** and ½ cup (1 stick) room-temperature **unsalted butter**, at room temperature, until fluffy, 1 to 2 minutes. Gradually beat in 4 cups **confectioners' sugar** until smooth. Beat in 1 tablespoon each **lime zest** and **lime juice**, 1 teaspoon **pure vanilla extract**, and 3 to 4 tablespoons **reserved strawberry puree**. ★

3	cups cake flour, spooned and leveled
1	teaspoon baking soda
1	teaspoon baking powder
¼	teaspoon salt
1	pound strawberries, chopped, plus more whole for garnish
½	cup buttermilk, at room temperature
1	cup (2 sticks) unsalted butter, at room temperature
1	cup granulated sugar
½	cup packed light brown sugar
3	large eggs, at room temperature
2	teaspoons pure vanilla extract
1	tablespoon lime zest

Strawberry-Cream Cheese Frosting (recipe at left)

1 Preheat oven to 350°F. Lightly spray three 8-inch round cake pans with cooking spray and line bottoms with parchment paper rounds. In bowl, whisk together flour, baking soda, baking powder, and salt.

2 In food processor, process strawberries until small pieces and a thick puree form, 5 to 10 seconds. In bowl, whisk together buttermilk and 1 cup strawberry puree. Reserve remaining puree for frosting.

3 With an electric mixer set on medium speed, beat butter and sugars until light and fluffy, 1 to 2 minutes. Add eggs, one at a time, beating well after each addition. Beat in vanilla and lime zest. Reduce speed to low and alternately beat in flour mixture and buttermilk mixture, starting and ending with flour mixture, just until flour is incorporated. Divide batter among prepared pans.

4 Bake until a toothpick inserted in center comes out clean, 20 to 23 minutes. Cool in pans on wire rack for 15 minutes, then invert onto rack to cool completely.

5 Place one layer on cake plate and frost top with 1 cup frosting. Repeat with remaining two layers. Cut 12" by 24" piece of plastic wrap and fold in half to make 6" by 24" strip. Wrap around cake to secure layers. Chill until frosting is set, 4 hours or up to 1 day. Top with whole strawberries just before serving.

SPECKLED MALTED COCONUT CAKE

This show-stopping treat should become a mainstay in your cake recipe arsenal. The three layers of fluffy white cake covered with a coconut buttercream frosting are almost too pretty to eat (but too delicious not to!).

ACTIVE TIME: 45 minutes
TOTAL TIME: 1 hour 30 minutes
MAKES: 12 to 15 servings

3   cups cake flour, spooned and leveled
1 ½ teaspoons baking powder
¼   cup malted milk powder
1   teaspoon salt
1   cup canola oil
1   cup half-and-half, at room temperature
1   cup granulated sugar
1   teaspoon pure vanilla extract
1   teaspoon pure coconut extract
1   large egg, at room temperature
2   large egg whites, at room temperature
Coconut Buttercream (recipe at right)
⅛   teaspoon brown gel food coloring
Phyllo Nest (recipe at right) and robin egg candies, for decorating

1 Preheat oven to 350°F. Lightly spray three 8-inch cake pans with cooking spray and line bottoms with parchment paper rounds. In bowl, whisk together flour, baking powder, malt powder, and salt.

2 In separate bowl, whisk together oil, half-and-half, sugar, vanilla, coconut extract, and egg until smooth. Fold in flour mixture just until incorporated. With an electric mixer set on medium-high speed, beat egg whites until stiff peaks form, 1 to 2 minutes. Fold egg whites into batter just until combined.

3 Divide batter among prepared pans. Bake until a toothpick inserted in center comes out clean, 18 to 22 minutes. Cool in pans on wire rack for 15 minutes, then invert onto racks to cool completely.

4 Place one layer on cake plate and frost top with 1 cup Coconut Buttercream. Repeat with remaining two layers. Frost sides with remaining Coconut Buttercream.

5 In small bowl, stir together food coloring and 2 drops water. Dip tip of wide stiff paintbrush into mixture. Holding brush 6 to 8 inches from cake, gently fling mixture onto iced cake. Repeat for desired effect. Spread Phyllo Nest around base of cake and nestle candies inside.

★ COCONUT BUTTERCREAM

With an electric mixer set on medium speed, beat 1 cup (2 sticks) room-temperature **unsalted butter** and ½ cup **cream of coconut** until smooth, 1 to 2 minutes. Gradually beat in 6 cups **confectioners' sugar**. Beat in 1 teaspoon **pure vanilla extract** and pinch **salt** until combined. Beat in **blue gel food coloring**, one drop at a time, to desired color.

★ PHYLLO NEST

Tightly toll 6 sheets **phyllo dough** lengthwise; very thinly slice. Transfer to baking sheet, loosely separating layers. Spray with **nonstick cooking spray**. Bake at 350°F until golden brown, 10 to 12 minutes. Cool completely.

SALTED CARAMEL PINEAPPLE UPSIDE-DOWN CAKE

This salty and sweet cake is perfect for any occasion.

ACTIVE TIME: 25 minutes
TOTAL TIME: 1 hour 35 minutes plus cooling
MAKES: 8 slices

1   cup dark brown sugar
1   cup (2 sticks) unsalted butter, at room temperature
3   tablespoons dark rum
1 ½ teaspoons salt
1 ½ cups all-purpose flour
2   teaspoons baking powder
½   teaspoon ground cinnamon
1   cup granulated sugar
1   tablespoon vanilla extract
2   large eggs
½   cup whole milk
1   medium pineapple, peeled, cored, and cut into rings
    (with 1 ring cut into chunks)

1 Coat 9-inch cake pan with cooking spray and set aside. In small saucepan, heat brown sugar and ½ cup butter over medium heat until sugar is dissolved, whisking occasionally. Bring to a boil and cook until caramel thickens and turns deep brown, about 3 minutes. Remove from heat and whisk in rum and 1 teaspoon salt. Pour caramel into prepared cake pan and swirl to coat. Set aside and let cool completely, at least 30 minutes.

2 Preheat oven to 350°F. In medium bowl, whisk together flour, baking powder, remaining ½ teaspoon salt, and cinnamon. In large bowl with electric mixer set on medium speed, beat together granulated sugar and remaining ½ cup butter until light and fluffy. Add vanilla and eggs, one at a time, beating well. Reduce speed to low and alternately beat dry ingredients and milk, starting and ending with dry ingredients.

3 Arrange pineapple rings on top of caramel in pan. Fill in spaces between rings with pineapple chunks. Carefully pour batter over pineapple and smooth with rubber spatula.

4 Bake until toothpick inserted in center comes out clean, about 50 minutes. Transfer pan to wire rack and let cool for 30 minutes. Run sharp knife around edges of pan to loosen cake; invert onto large serving plate.

ALMOND & POPPY SEED LOAF CAKE

Things are about to get really exciting in your old loaf pan.

ACTIVE TIME: 30 minutes
TOTAL TIME: 1 hour 30 minutes
MAKES: 8 servings

1 ½ cups all-purpose flour, spooned and leveled
½ teaspoon baking powder
½ teaspoon salt
½ cup (1 stick) unsalted butter, at room temperature
1 cup granulated sugar
3 large eggs, at room temperature
1 teaspoon pure vanilla extract
½ teaspoon pure almond extract
½ cup whole milk, at room temperature
2 tablespoons poppy seeds
Almond Glaze (recipe below)

1 Preheat oven to 325°F. Lightly spray 8" by 4" loaf pan. In bowl, whisk together flour, baking powder, and salt.

2 With an electric mixer set on medium speed, beat butter and sugar until light and fluffy, 1 to 2 minutes. Add eggs, one at a time, beating well after each addition. Beat in vanilla and almond extracts. Reduce speed to low and alternately beat in flour mixture and milk, starting and ending with flour mixture, just until flour is incorporated. Fold in poppy seeds. Pour batter into prepared pan.

3 Bake until toothpick inserted in center comes out clean, 45 to 55 minutes. Cool in pan on wire rack for 15 minutes, and then remove to rack to cool completely.

4 Drizzle cooled cake with Almond Glaze.

★ ALMOND GLAZE

In bowl, whisk together 1 cup **confectioners' sugar**, 1 ½ tablespoons **milk**, ½ teaspoon each **pure vanilla extract** and **pure almond extract**, and pinch **salt**. Add additional **milk**, 1 teaspoon at a time, to reach desired consistency. ★

LADY GREY CUPCAKES WITH ORANGE ZEST FROSTING

Tea time just got a whole lot livlier with these citrusy frosted cupcakes.

ACTIVE TIME: 45 minutes
TOTAL TIME: 1 hour 30 minutes
MAKES: 20 cupcakes

3   cups all-purpose flour, spooned and leveled
1   teaspoon baking powder
½   teaspoon baking soda
½   teaspoon salt
3   bags Lady Grey tea
¼   cup pure honey
1½ cups granulated sugar, divided
1   cup half-and-half
1   cup (2 sticks) unsalted butter, at room temperature
2   large eggs
1   teaspoon pure vanilla extract
Orange Zest Frosting (recipe below)

1 Preheat oven to 350°F. Line 20 standard muffin cups with paper liners. In bowl, whisk together flour, baking powder, baking soda, and salt.

2 In small saucepan, bring ½ cup water to a simmer; add tea bags and steep for 10 minutes. Squeeze tea bags to remove excess liquid; discard bags. Stir in honey and ¼ cup sugar until dissolved. In bowl, stir together ¼ cup tea syrup and half-and-half. Reserve remaining syrup.

3 With an electric mixer set on medium speed, beat butter and remaining 1¼ cups sugar until light and fluffy, 1 to 2 minutes. Add eggs, one at a time, beating well after each addition. Beat in vanilla. Reduce speed to low and alternately beat in flour mixture and half-and-half mixture, starting and ending with flour mixture, just until flour is incorporated. Divide batter evenly among prepared muffin cups.

4 Bake until a toothpick inserted in center comes out clean, 18 to 20 minutes. Use toothpick to poke 10 holes in top of each cupcake and brush with remaining tea syrup. Cool completely in pans on wire rack.

5 Frost cooled cupcakes with Orange Zest Frosting.

★ ORANGE ZEST FROSTING

With an electric mixer set on medium speed, beat 1 cup (2 sticks) room-temperature **unsalted butter** and 16 ounces **confectioners' sugar** until smooth, 1 to 2 minutes. Beat in 1 tablespoon **orange zest**, 2 tablespoons each **orange juice** and **milk**, and pinch **salt** until ★ smooth.

S'MORES COOKIES

Turn the classic campfire treat on its head by taking summer's favorite dessert ingredients and transforming them into a delectably ooey-gooey cookie.

ACTIVE TIME: 30 minutes
TOTAL TIME: 1 hour 10 minutes
MAKES: 18 cookies

2	cups all-purpose flour
10	graham crackers, crushed to fine crumbs
1	teaspoon baking soda
1	teaspoon salt
1	cup (2 sticks) unsalted butter, softened
½	cup granulated sugar
½	cup dark brown sugar
1	teaspoon pure vanilla extract
2	large eggs
8	ounces dark chocolate chips
2	ounces marshmallow crème
2¼	teaspoons flaky sea salt

1 Preheat oven to 350°F. Line two baking sheets with parchment paper.

2 In large bowl, whisk together flour, graham cracker crumbs, baking soda, and salt; set aside.

3 With an electric mixer, cream together butter and sugars until pale and fluffy, 2 to 3 minutes. Add vanilla and eggs, one at a time, beating well after each addition. Add flour mixture and beat until just combined.

4 Drop dough in 2-tablespoon portions onto prepared baking sheets. Lightly press down to flatten to ½-inch thickness. Bake for 14 to 15 minutes or until golden brown around edges. Let cool on baking sheet for 5 minutes; transfer to wire rack to cool completely.

5 In small heatproof bowl set over small saucepan simmering water, melt chocolate until smooth, stirring often; let cool for 2 to 4 minutes. Using spoon or spatula, spread each cookie with 1 heaping teaspoon marshmallow crème. Drizzle 1 teaspoon melted chocolate on top of crème and swirl together. Sprinkle immediately with salt. Let harden for 30 minutes before serving.

TRIPLE CHOCOLATE-HAZELNUT COOKIES

These cookies make a great edible gift! Just stack four cookies in a clear plastic bag and tie with decorative ribbon.

ACTIVE TIME: 20 minutes
TOTAL TIME: 1 hour 45 minutes
MAKES: about 4 dozen cookies

3 ½ cups all-purpose flour, spooned and leveled

1   cup granulated sugar

1   cup packed light brown sugar

2   teaspoons baking powder

1   teaspoon salt

½   teaspoon baking soda

½   teaspoon instant coffee powder

1   cup cocoa powder

¾   cup canola oil

¾   cup chocolate-hazelnut spread

2   large eggs, at room temperature

1   teaspoon pure vanilla extract

1 ½ cups coarsely chopped bittersweet chocolate

1   cup coarsely chopped toasted hazelnuts

2   teaspoons flaked sea salt

1 Preheat oven to 350°F with racks arranged in upper and lower thirds of oven. Line two baking sheets with parchment paper. In bowl, whisk together flour, sugars, baking powder, salt, baking soda, and coffee.

2 With an electric mixer set on low speed, beat cocoa, oil, hazelnut spread, and ¾ cup warm water until combined, about 30 seconds. Add eggs, one at a time, beating well after each addition. Beat in vanilla. Stir flour mixture into cocoa mixture just until incorporated. Stir in chocolate and hazelnuts.

3 Drop dough in 2-tablespoon portions on prepared baking sheets, spacing 3 inches apart; sprinkle with sea salt. Bake until dry around the edges, 12 to 14 minutes, rotating sheets halfway through baking. Cool on baking sheets on wire racks for 10 minutes, and then remove to racks to cool completely.

LEMON MERINGUE PIE

This recipe sticks with tradition, resulting in a decadent pie that'll hit the spot every time with a smooth filling, airy meringue, and buttery crust.

ACTIVE TIME: 25 minutes
TOTAL TIME: 3 hours 15 minutes
MAKES: 8 servings

1	refrigerated ready-to-bake pie crust
1 1/3	cups plus 3/4 cup granulated sugar
1/3	cup cornstarch
5	large eggs, yolks and whites separated
1	tablespoon grated lemon zest, plus 1/2 cup fresh lemon juice
2	tablespoons cold butter
1/2	teaspoon cream of tartar

1 Preheat oven to 450°F. Coat 9-inch pie plate with nonstick cooking spray. Fit crust into pie plate; freeze for 15 minutes. Prebake crust as box directs. Remove pie plate to wire rack. Reduce oven temperature to 350°F.

2 In 2-quart saucepan, combine 1 1/3 cups sugar and cornstarch. Whisk in 1 1/2 cups lukewarm water, egg yolks, and lemon juice. Bring to a gentle boil and cook for 1 minute, until translucent and thick, stirring. Remove from heat; stir in zest and butter until butter melts. Pour into crust.

3 In a large bowl with an electric mixer set on low speed, beat egg whites and cream of tartar until soft peaks form. Increase speed to medium-high and add remaining 3/4 cup sugar, 1 tablespoon at a time, beating just until stiff peaks form when beaters are lifted (do not overbeat). Spoon meringue on top of pie filling, mounding in center and spreading to edges of crust. Swirl meringue decoratively.

4 Bake until browned and an instant-read thermometer inserted in meringue registers at least 160°F, 20 minutes. Cool completely, and then refrigerate for at least 2 hours before serving.

SALTY PEANUT BANANA PUDDING

The best part of this salty-and-sweet dessert? You don't have to bake it!

ACTIVE TIME: 25 minutes
TOTAL TIME: 4 hours 25 minutes
MAKES: 8 servings

1/3 cup all-purpose flour, spooned and leveled
1/4 teaspoon salt
2/3 cup plus 3 tablespoons granulated sugar
1 3/4 cups whole milk
4 large egg yolks
1 3/4 cups heavy cream, divided
1/3 cup creamy peanut butter
3 teaspoons pure vanilla extract, divided
50 vanilla wafers
4 medium ripe bananas, sliced
3/4 cup chopped roasted and salted peanuts, divided

1 In medium saucepan, whisk together flour, salt, and 2/3 cup sugar. Whisk in milk, egg yolks, and 1/2 cup cream. Cook over medium heat until thickened with a pudding-like consistency, 7 to 9 minutes, stirring constantly. Remove from heat and whisk in peanut butter and 2 teaspoons vanilla.

2 In bottom of 8" by 8" baking dish, arrange 25 wafers, overlapping slightly. Top with half of banana slices, 1/4 cup peanuts, and hot pudding.
Top with remaining bananas, 25 wafers, and 1/4 cup peanuts. Cover and chill for 4 hours or up to overnight.

3 With an electric mixer set on medium-high, beat remaining 3 tablespoons sugar, 1 1/4 cups cream, and 1 teaspoon vanilla just until stiff peaks form, 2 to 3 minutes. Spread over top. Sprinkle with remaining 1/4 cup peanuts.

ALMOND, PEACH & BLUEBERRY COBBLER

This sweet treat brings the flavor with tons of peaches and blueberries.

ACTIVE TIME: 20 minutes
TOTAL TIME: 1 hour 5 minutes
MAKES: 6 to 8 servings

★ YEAR-ROUND COBBLER CRUST

In bowl, stir together 1 ½ cups (spooned and leveled) **all-purpose flour**, 2 tablespoons **granulated sugar**, and ½ teaspoon **salt**. With two forks or pastry blender, cut ¼ cup (½ stick) **unsalted butter** into flour mixture until it resembles coarse meal. In separate bowl, whisk together ¼ cup **milk** and 1 large **egg yolk**. Add milk mixture to flour mixture and stir with fork until crumbly. Sprinkle dough over desired filling or knead until dough comes together, 3 to 4 times; pat to ½-inch thickness and cut into rounds or squares and place on ★ desired filling.

2	tablespoons unsalted butter, cut up, plus more for pan
4	cups diced fresh peaches
2	cups fresh blueberries
½	cup granulated sugar
¼	cup all-purpose flour
1	tablespoon lemon zest
1	teaspoon pure vanilla extract
½	teaspoon pure almond extract
¼	teaspoon salt

Year-Round Cobbler Crust (recipe at left)

1 Preheat oven to 425°F. Lightly butter 8" by 8" baking pan.

2 In bowl, stir together butter, peaches, blueberries, sugar, flour, lemon zest, vanilla and almond extracts, and salt; transfer to prepared pan. Top with Year-Round Cobbler Crust.

3 Bake until crust is golden brown and mixture is bubbly, 40 to 45 minutes. Cool for 10 minutes before serving.

MINTED STRAWBERRY RHUBARB COBBLER

Ring in spring with this tart and easy to assemble minty strawberry cobbler.

ACTIVE TIME: 20 minutes
TOTAL TIME: 1 hour 5 minutes
MAKES: 6 to 8 servings

2	tablespoons unsalted butter, cut up, plus more for pan
4	cups halved strawberries
2	cups sliced rhubarb
½	cup granulated sugar
¼	cup all-purpose flour
3	tablespoons chopped fresh mint
2	teaspoons pure vanilla extract
¼	teaspoon salt

Year-Round Cobber Crust (recipe opposite)

1 Preheat oven to 425°F. Lightly butter 8" by 8" baking pan.

2 In bowl, stir together butter, strawberries, rhubarb, sugar, flour, mint, vanilla, and salt; transfer to prepared baking pan. Top with Year-Round Cobbler Crust.

3 Bake until crust is golden brown and mixture is bubbly, 40 to 45 minutes. Cool for 10 minutes before serving.

Butter by the Numbers

Baking recipes usually call for butter by the cup or tablespoon. Use this chart to determine how many sticks you'll need.

CUPS	TABLESPOONS	STICKS	CUPS	TABLESPOONS	STICKS
¼	4	½	1¼	20	2½
½	8	1	1½	24	3
¾	12	1½	1¾	28	3½
1	16	2	2	32	4

CLASSIC VANILLA ICE CREAM

It's a cold hard fact: This foolproof vanilla recipe is the perfect blank slate for multiple mix-ins.

ACTIVE TIME: 20 minutes
TOTAL TIME: 9 hours 35 minutes
MAKES: 8 servings

3	cups whole milk
2	cups heavy cream
½	cup sugar
¼	teaspoon salt
1	vanilla bean, halved lengthwise
5	large egg yolks

1 In large heavy saucepan, whisk together milk, cream, sugar, salt, and vanilla bean. Cook over medium heat until sugar dissolves and mixture is hot, 4 minutes, stirring often. Gradually whisk about 1 cup hot milk mixture into egg yolks; whisk yolk mixture into remaining milk mixture. Cook over medium heat until mixture thickens and coats back of spoon, 8 to 10 minutes, whisking constantly.

2 Pour through fine wire-mesh strainer into bowl, discarding solids. Cool completely. Chill for 8 to 24 hours or until very cold.

3 Pour mixture into bowl of electric ice-cream maker and process according to manufacturer's instructions. Freeze for 1 hour before serving. Store for up to 1 week.

Variations

CRUNCHY CINNAMON: Stir in 2 teaspoons ground cinnamon with sugar in step 1 and 2 cups crumbled cinnamon-sugar toasted cereal into prepared ice cream before freezing in step 3.

TRIPLE CHOCOLATE BROWNIE: Whisk in $\frac{1}{3}$ cup unsweetened cocoa with sugar in step 1. Stir in $\frac{1}{2}$ cup milk chocolate morsels and 1 finely chopped bar (3.5 ounces) dark chocolate into warm ice-cream base until chocolates are melted before chilling in step 2. Swirl 1 $\frac{1}{2}$ cups finely chopped fudge brownies and $\frac{2}{3}$ cup chocolate fudge sauce into prepared ice cream before freezing in step 3.

PEANUT BUTTER BUCKEYE: Stir $\frac{3}{4}$ cup creamy peanut butter into hot ice-cream base before chilling in step 2. Swirl $\frac{1}{2}$ cup chocolate fudge sauce and $\frac{1}{2}$ cup finely chopped honey-roasted peanuts into prepared ice cream before freezing in step 3.

COCONUT MACAROON: Reduce cream to 1 cup. Stir in 1 (14-ounce) can light coconut milk with milk in step 1. Stir 1 cup toasted sweetened flaked coconut into ice-cream base before chilling in step 2 and 1 $\frac{1}{2}$ cups crumbled coconut macaroons into prepared ice cream before freezing in step 3.

PEPPERMINT PATTY: Stir in 20 crushed peppermints with sugar in step 1. Swirl $\frac{1}{2}$ cup chocolate fudge sauce and 1 $\frac{1}{4}$ cups finely chopped peppermint patties into prepared ice cream before freezing in step 3.

INDULGENT GELATO

Craving a slightly more adventurous dessert? Try this decadent Italian treat pronto.

ACTIVE TIME: 25 minutes
TOTAL TIME: 9 hours 40 minutes
MAKES: 8 servings

²/₃	cup granulated sugar
2	tablespoons cornstarch
¼	teaspoon salt
3	cups heavy cream
2	cups whole milk
1	vanilla bean, halved lengthwise
8	large egg yolks

1 In large heavy saucepan, whisk together sugar, cornstarch, and salt. Whisk in cream, milk, and vanilla bean. Cook over medium heat until sugar dissolves, 4 minutes, stirring often. Gradually whisk 1 cup hot cream mixture into egg yolks. Whisk egg yolk mixture into remaining cream mixture. Cook over medium heat until mixture thickens and coats back of spoon, 8 to 10 minutes, whisking constantly.

2 Pour through fine wire-mesh strainer into bowl, discarding solids. Cool completely. Chill for 8 to 24 hours or until very cold.

3 Pour mixture into bowl of electric ice-cream maker; process according to manufacturer's instructions. Freeze for 1 hour before serving. Store for up to 1 week.

Variations

NANNERNUTTER FLUFF: Stir 2 mashed, very ripe **bananas** and ⅓ cup **creamy peanut butter** into warm gelato base before chilling in step 2. Swirl ½ cup **marshmallow topping** into prepared gelato before freezing in step 3.

ARMAGNAC FIG & SALTY CARAMEL: Soak 1½ cups finely chopped **dried figs** in 1 cup **Armagnac brandy** for 1 hour; drain. Swirl figs, ¾ cup **butterscotch caramel sauce**, and ½ teaspoon **sea salt** into prepared gelato before freezing in step 3.

GOAT CHEESE & PEACH: In saucepan, cook 2 ½ cups diced **fresh peaches** and ¼ cup **granulated sugar** until softened; cool completely. Stir 6 ounces crumbled **goat cheese** and 2 teaspoons **peach schnapps** into prepared gelato before chilling in step 2. Swirl cooked peach mixture into prepared gelato before freezing in step 3.

BUTTERMILK SWEET CORN: In food processor, pulse 2 cups cooked and cooled fresh **sweet corn kernels** and ¼ teaspoon **salt** until creamy but still slightly coarse. Stir corn mixture and ¾ cup **whole buttermilk** into prepared gelato before chilling in step 2.

BITTERSWEET CHOCOLATE: Stir in ⅓ cup **unsweetened cocoa** with sugar in step 1. Whisk ⅔ cup **bittersweet chocolate morsels** into prepared gelato until chocolate is melted before chilling in step 2.

INDEX

Note: Page numbers in italics indicate photos separate from recipes.

PHOTOGRAPHY CREDITS

METRIC CONVERSION CHARTS

The recipes that appear in this cookbook use the standard United States method for measuring liquid and dry or solid ingredients (teaspoons, tablespoons, and cups). The information on this chart is provided to help cooks outside the U.S. successfully use these recipes. All equivalents are approximate.

METRIC EQUIVALENTS FOR DIFFERENT TYPES OF INGREDIENTS

STANDARD CUP	FINE POWDER (e.g. flour)	GRAIN (e.g. rice)	GRANULAR (e.g. sugar)	LIQUID SOLIDS (e.g. butter)	LIQUID (e.g. milk)
¾	105 g	113 g	143 g	150 g	180 ml
⅔	93 g	100 g	125 g	133 g	160 ml
½	70 g	75 g	95 g	100 g	120 ml
⅓	47 g	50 g	63 g	67 g	80 ml
¼	35 g	38 g	48 g	50 g	60 ml
⅛	18 g	19 g	24 g	25 g	30 ml

USEFUL EQUIVALENTS FOR LIQUID INGREDIENTS BY VOLUME

¼ tsp	=						1 ml		
½ tsp	=						2 ml		
1 tsp	=						5 ml		
3 tsp	=	1 tbls	=			½ fl oz	=	15 ml	
		2 tbls	=	⅛ cup	=	1 fl oz	=	30 ml	
		4 tbls	=	¼ cup	=	2 fl oz	=	60 ml	
		5 ⅓ tbls	=	⅓ cup	=	3 fl oz	=	80 ml	
		8 tbls	=	½ cup	=	4 fl oz	=	120 ml	
		10 ⅔ tbls	=	⅔ cup	=	5 fl oz	=	160 ml	
		12 tbls	=	¾ cup	=	6 fl oz	=	180 ml	
		16 tbls	=	1 cup	=	8 fl oz	=	240 ml	
		1 pt	=	2 cups	=	16 fl oz	=	480 ml	
		1 qt	=	4 cups	=	32 fl oz	=	960 ml	
						33 fl oz	=	1000 ml	= 1 L

USEFUL EQUIVALENTS FOR DRY INGREDIENTS BY WEIGHT

(To convert ounces to grams, multiply the number of ounces by 30.)

1 oz	=	¹⁄₁₆ lb	=	30 g
4 oz	=	¼ lb	=	120 g
8 oz	=	½ lb	=	240 g
12 oz	=	¾ lb	=	360 g
16 oz	=	1 lb	=	480 g

USEFUL EQUIVALENTS FOR COOKING/OVEN TEMPERATURES

	FAHRENHEIT	CELSIUS	GAS MARK
Freeze Water	32º F	0º C	
Room Temperature	68º F	20º C	
Boil Water	212º F	100º C	
Bake	325º F	160º C	3
	350º F	180º C	4
	375º F	190º C	5
	400º F	200º C	6
	425º F	220º C	7
	450º F	230º C	8
Broil			Grill

USEFUL EQUIVALENTS LENGTH

(To convert inches to centimeters, multiply the number of inches by 2.5.)

1 in =		2.5 cm	
6 in = ½ ft =		15 cm	
12 in = 1 ft =		30 cm	
36 in = 3 ft = 1 yd =	90 cm		
40 in =		100 cm	= 1 m

HEARSTBOOKS

An Imprint of Sterling Publishing Co., Inc.
1166 Avenue of the Americas
New York, NY 10036

ISBN 978-1-61837-235-2

Distributed in Canada by Sterling Publishing Co., Inc.
c/o Canadian Manda Group, 664 Annette Street
Toronto, Ontario, Canada M6S 2C8
Distributed in Australia by NewSouth Books
45 Beach Street, Coogee, NSW 2034, Australia

For information about custom editions, special sales, and premium
and corporate purchases, please contact Sterling Special Sales at
800-805-5489 or specialsales@sterlingpublishing.com.

Manufactured in China

2 4 6 8 10 9 7 5 3 1

www.sterlingpublishing.com

Design by Anna Christian